COUNTRY INNS

ONTARIO'S BEST GETAWAYS

COUNTRY INNS

ONTARIO'S BEST GETAWAYS

Donna Carpenter

The BOSTON
MILLS PRESS

APPRECIATION

I am deeply indebted to the innkeepers and staff at all of the inns included in this book. Not only did they allow me to interrupt their busy schedules, but they gave me complete access to their properties. Their gracious hospitality was appreciated, and their outstanding contribution to tourism in Ontario is an inspiration. Thank you to one and all.

Published in 1997 by
Boston Mills Press
www.boston-mills.on.ca

Distributed in Canada by
General Distribution Services Inc.
30 Lesmill Road
Toronto, Canada M3B 2T6
Tel 416-445-3333
Fax 416-445-5967
e-mail customer.service@ccmailgw.genpub.com

Distributed in the United States by
General Distribution Services Inc.
85 River Rock Drive, Suite 202
Buffalo, New York 14207
Toll-free 1-800-805-1083
Fax 416-445-5967
e-mail gdsinc.genpub.com

01 00 99 98 97   2 3 4 5

Cataloging in Publication Data

Carpenter, Donna May Gibbs, 1954–
Country inns : Ontario's best getaways

ISBN 1-55046-236-9

1. Hotels - Ontario - Guidebooks.   I. Title

Cover, text design and illustrations by Mary Firth
Editing by James Bosma
Printed in Canada

Contents

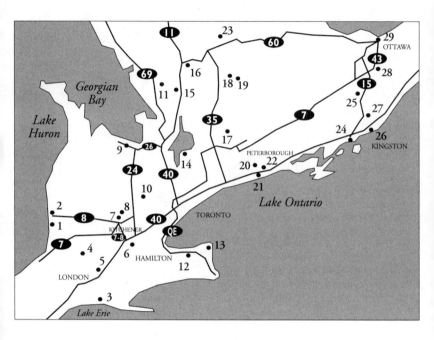

COUNTRY INNS

ONTARIO'S BEST GETAWAYS

1. The Little Inn of Bayfield
2. Benmiller Inn
3. Kettle Creek Inn
4. Westover Inn
5. Elm Hurst Inn
6. Langdon Hall
7. Jakobstettel Guest House
8. The Elora Mill Inn
9. Beild House Country Inn
10. The Millcroft Inn
11. Sherwood Inn
12. The Vintner's Inn
13. The Kiely Inn & Restaurant
14. The Briars
15. Inn at the Falls
16. Grandview
17. Eganridge Inn & Country Club
18. Sir Sam's Inn
19. Domain of Killien
20. The Victoria Inn
21. Woodlawn Terrace Inn
22. Ste. Anne's Country Inn & Spa
23. Arowhon Pines
24. Rosemount Bed & Breakfast Inn
25. Gallagher House
26. Trinity House Inn
27. Denaut Mansion Country Inn
28. Sam Jakes Inn
29. The Carmichael Inn & Spa

INTRODUCTION

Ontario has a great deal to offer travellers. My previous work has been dedicated to revealing that our museums, nature preserves, theatres and historic villages can compete with the best tourist attractions on this continent. A large number of inns exist in Ontario, and I began to wonder whether our inns were of the same high calibre.

After spending several months relishing the warm hospitality of Ontario's country inns, I am now convinced that, next to Ontario's spectacular scenery, our inns are our best tourism resource. I was touched by the courtesy and grace of the innkeepers, delighted by the creativity of the chefs, impressed at the attention to detail of the staff, and charmed with the loveliness of these deeply historic properties.

I have selected the inns in this book according to the following criteria. First, each inn has an interesting location, set in either an area of natural beauty, or a village of historic interest. Second, each inn has its own interesting history. I have included a diversity of intriguing buildings — a stone mill, winery warehouse, a seminary — all enjoying second careers as inns. Third, each inn provides attentive service. Finally, each inn is attractive, functional and distinctive.

An inn is a manifestation of the philosophy of the individual innkeeper and of the character of the surrounding region. An inn begins with the vision of one person. That vision is clarified as the inn's niche in the tourism market is defined and as the business matures and develops a regional outlook. This influence of the natural or cultural environment is expressed in many ways, including locally produced foodstuffs on the menu, regional naturalists and artists leading weekend workshops, events to promote local charities, and efforts at environmental stewardship.

This book describes twenty-nine of Ontario's best inns. With the exception of two excellent newly opened inns, most of these inns have been operating for a long time. (A good inn, like a flourishing garden, takes time to develop and mature, and I generally wanted to include time-tested properties.) I have also tried to cover a large geographic area, with properties from Lake Huron to the Rideau valley, and from Algonquin Park to Niagara.

The inns selected offer a wide range of facilities. Some inns are small kingdoms unto themselves, with a full range of recreation facilities. Others have few on-site amenities, and are better used as a home base for an exploration of their surrounding region. Many innkeepers are willing to help you plan daytrips or make arrangements for special activities such as golf, cycling, canoeing, or an evening of theatre.

A similar wide range of facilities and decor is available in the guest rooms. Some offer exquisitely appointed spacious suites with large en suite bathrooms, while others have a simple, homey decor and shared bathroom facilities. You will be able to determine this from the written descriptions and choose the type of setting that best suites your taste. If you have specific requirements, such as dietary restrictions or mobility challenges, or if you can't live without a television or an exercise room, ask the inn at the time of booking whether these special needs can be met.

Price is often a consideration when choosing an inn. I have provided a general description of prices, using three categories: inexpensive, moderate and expensive. This was determined on the cost of weekend for two, including meals and accommodations. A weekend at an inexpensive inn costs less than $400; inns in the moderate category will charge between $400 and $550; and you can expect to pay over $550 at an expensive inn. These price ranges are estimates, however, and many inns offer midweek and off-season specials that will reduce the cost of a stay. On the other hand, you will end up paying a good deal more than these prices if you order the best bottle of wine in the house and sleep in the choicest suite. The price estimates include accommodation, breakfast and dinner; for those inns that do not serve dinner, the cost of a meal at a local restaurant was included.

Don't think of Ontario's inns only when planning a leisure trip. All of the inns in this book are suited to business meetings. The smaller inns are best suited for executive retreats and small meetings, while the larger inns can provide excellent facilities for conferences and large corporate groups. The same personal service, excellent facilities and inventive cuisine that one can expect from an inn holiday can be expected for a corporate event.

No matter what the motivation is for your getaway — a romantic weekend, a few days of quiet repose, or some time to explore the countryside — there is a perfect inn out there waiting to give you the time of your life.

THE LITTLE INN OF BAYFIELD

Bayfield

The Little Inn is the perfect image of a country inn, and as such, its photograph has appeared in numerous publications. Sepia-tone photographs of the inn from the early 1800s show a square, pale-brick building with a widow's walk, a broad wrap-around porch and an upper-storey verandah. Stagecoaches and drivers are stationed out front, and guests mingle on the porch. The modern scene has changed so little — with the exception of the coach and horses and the addition of huge weeping willows that gently caress the verandah — that a stay at this inn will make you feel as though you've stepped back in time.

Much of the inn's charm owes to its wonderful porch. The square, olive-green pillars have ornate white brackets, the railings are green with white pickets, and hanging baskets of bright red impatiens add accent colour. But the inside is equally charming. Double front doors, trimmed with garlands and large red bows during the holiday season, and flanked by antique croquet chairs during the summer, lead into a truly congenial guest parlour. The inn is decorated in period furnishings and heritage colours. The parlour has a settee and plenty of armchairs for guests who wish to while away a few hours, and there is an antique square grand piano for those who like to tickle the ivories.

Thirty-one guest rooms are available on the upper storey of the main inn and in the Little Inn Guest Cottage located a few houses away. The rooms are decorated to period. A flatiron acts as a door stop, lace curtains cover the windows, rocking chairs sit next to the fireplace, and the beds are covered with fluffy white duvets. Some beds have deeply carved headboards; one room even has a magnificent bird's-eye maple sleigh bed that is highly prized by antique lovers. Given the view of the historic main street and the decor of the rooms, you will swear that you've been trans-ported back a century.

Every room has a terrific view. Those facing Main Street look out past the inviting wooden chairs on the balcony to the board-

and-batten storefronts along the sidewalk. The rooms at the rear of the house face the gardens, rich in bloom all season long, where there are Muskoka chairs and a bocce court. The "Widow's Walk" room has the best panorama of all. It is a bi-level suite, with a bed on the lower level and a cozy sitting room up in the rooftop widow's walk (a glassed-in room where women used to watch for returning sailors). The widow's walk is a prime location for surveying the street or enjoying one of those famous Lake Huron sunsets.

Further guest accommodations are located just down the street in the recently constructed guest cottage. The Cottage is a large, pine-sided vacation house set among huge walnut trees. Social and corporate groups sometimes use the rustic, spacious sunken lounge. With its stone flooring, antiques, double-sided fieldstone fireplace, and prints of early Canadian scenes, it is the perfect meeting place. The picturesque backyard garden, with a circular flagstone patio arranged in blue patio furniture, is some-times used as an outdoor wedding chapel.

All of the rooms in the Little Inn Cottage are well appointed, with fireplaces and private decks or balconies. The decor, more contemporary than at the inn, is even more luxurious. The Florence Walter suite is highly recommended. Its main-floor liv-ing room has a fireplace and a walkout to a private deck. In the bathroom is a huge sunken whirlpool tub, and in the bedroom, a tall, rounded window that faces the garden.

Meals are served in two dining rooms on the main floor of the inn. Small tables and ladderback chairs, white linens and fresh flowers set the scene for fine cuisine. The older dining room is dec-orated with tri-tone sketches taken from photographs of old Bayfield. They were created by senior art club students at Clinton High School, who worked with conté pencils to achieve the look of oil pastels. The sketches are so true to life that village residents have identified friends and relatives in the scenes. The adjacent dining room is in an addition that joins the inn to its neighbouring carriage house. The yellow-brick walls, terra cotta flooring, and floor-to-ceiling windows correspond well with the old building.

Another popular room at the inn is the pub, which serves the usual potent potables, including ales and lagers by Glatt, a London, Ontario-based microbrewery. The pub's specialty, though, is its stock of over twenty varieties of single malt whiskeys, which represent each of Scotland's regions. Next to the bar is a games room, where guests can enjoy a rubber of bridge or a game of chess next to the fireplace. There is an antique organ in this room that was made in Guelph in 1898; its foot pedals are labelled "mouse proof."

The kitchen staff is led by Richard Fitoussi, who gained his expertise in food and wine in France and Germany. Sweet yellow tomatoes are combined with goat cheese, adzuki beans and garden-fresh herbs, in a heavenly salad. The house specialty is an appetizer of wild boar, lake trout, and cold smoked venison, which is served with garden greens and the inn's own eight-grain bread.

Main courses are inventively presented. Roast breast of pheasant is accented with juniper berries, cranberries and porto sauce; and chicken breast, stuffed with Asiago cheese and Westphalian ham, floats on a tomato, red pepper and sweet corn salsa. Huron County prides itself on its delicious beef, which the Little Inn serves many ways, including entrecôte striploin, with mushrooms and shallots, in which the beef is topped with savoury sautéed marrow.

For dessert, two classic Canadian tastes are combined in a tart of sun-dried wild blueberries cooked with walnuts and maple syrup. Another irresistible dessert is called "tic-tac-toe:" chocolate drizzle is used to create a game board, and three ambrosial sweets — a small crème caramel, a chocolate truffle and a frozen maple cream encased in a marzipan bell — represent playing pieces.

The Little Inn's wine list recently won the *Wine Spectator*'s award for the quality of its 150 wines. The extensive list — with a broad selection from Canada, Europe, the United and Australia — includes a detailed description of each wine written by Fitoussi and including comments from other experts.

Several special dining events are noted prominently on the calendars of regular patrons. True to its roots as a commercial fishing port, Bayfield has six fishing boats that ply the waters of Lake Huron. The inn celebrates the town's heritage with a fish festival. The menu, depending on the bounty of the catch, may include an appetizer of cold smoked trout, followed by pickerel cheeks in puff pastry, and whitefish quenelles in a saffron cream sauce.

The Wine and Dine weekends held in February are a highlight of winter in Bayfield. Six wine-enhanced courses are offered, with such dishes as scallops in a champagne broth and grilled loin of lamb bordelaise. Each course is accompanied with a specially selected wine, including Gold Medal winners from Canadian and European competitions. Fitoussi also leads weekend cooking workshops on food preparation and choice of quality ingredients.

(Other weekend programs are also offered, include gardening and investment seminars.)

The Little Inn is a well-established part of the Huron shore community, and innkeepers Gayle and Patrick Waters are very familiar with their locale. Jim Francis, a fifth-generation Bayfielder, who knows area woods and streams better than most of us know our own backyards, has been a special find for the Waters. Francis takes inn guests out to search for wild foods, to observe migrating waterfowl at the Hullett Wildlife Area, and to track deer across frozen Naftel's Creek. These outings include transportation, amply stocked picnic baskets, and any required equipment. The Bayfield River is habitat for several species of game fish, among them steelhead, smallmouth bass and salmon. Fly-fisherman Ken Amoral guides inn guests on full-day fishing expeditions, and even supplies equipment.

The town of Bayfield has several opportunities for outdoor activities. Level roads and smooth pavement make for superb inline skating, and Tory's, across the street from the inn, sells and rents all of the necessary gear. Cross-country skiers also appreciate the village's quiet streets; some guests strap on their skis on the front porch and cruise along the side streets. The innkeepers can help cyclists plan country-roads tours. A popular plan is to ride from the Little Inn to Zurich, take lunch at the pub, and then return to Bayfield along a different route.

But Bayfield is first and foremost a lake town. The beach and marina are the main attraction for most travellers; the beach is great for swimming and windsurfing, and the marina rents canoes and paddleboats. Fishing and sailing charters can be arranged, and boat cruises are offered during the summer, including a sunset trip.

Main Street has dozens of inviting boutiques. All shops sell quality merchandise — no tacky souvenirs here — and several deserve special mention. You can meet all your gift-shopping needs at Avanti-Leser (functional and decorative works in clay and glass), Gammages (gardening), the Croft and the Bayberry (handicrafts), and The Wardrobe (top-quality Canadian fashions). The lover of old furnishings and country accents will want to visit Times & Places and Pineridge Country House.

Theatregoers may want to take in a play at either the Blyth Festival, in Blyth, or the Huron County Playhouse, in Grand Bend. The former has a solid reputation for original Canadian works that often go on to celebrity in larger centres, and the latter presents musicals, comedies and mysteries. The Lambton Heritage Museum is also located in Grand Bend. The museum is comprised of a main building, with displays on local pioneer history, and several outdoor exhibits, which include a pioneer church and agricultural machinery. Pressed-glass decanters and nineteenth-century hand-coloured lithographs are museum specialties.

The Little Inn welcomes guests to sample the best of two centuries. Luxuriate in the atmosphere of a stagecoach inn, land the first trout of spring, and then enjoy a new production before it opens in Toronto. Time travel couldn't be more appealing.

The Little Inn of Bayfield

Box 100
Bayfield, ON
N0M 1G0
(519) 565-2611
1-800-565-1832
Fax: (519) 565-5474
Innkeepers: Gayle and Patrick Waters, Richard Fitoussi

31 rooms in two buildings
Dining room open to the public
Directions: Bayfield is on Highway 21, south of Goderich.
Tariffs: moderate
On site: gardens, bocce court
Off site: Blyth Festival, Huron County Playhouse, Lambton
    County Museum, Huron County Pioneer Museum,
    shopping, antique hunting, country drives, boating, fishing,
    fly-fishing, beaches, windsurfing, cross-country skiing

BENMILLER INN

Benmiller

Maybe it's the water that does it — the babbling, mesmerizing music of Sharpe's Creek as it tumbles over rocks. Or perhaps it's the tranquil waters of the mill pond, reflecting puffy Huron County clouds, that pulls your thoughts away from the daily grind. Whatever it is, Benmiller is an effective antidote to the hassle and hustle of modern life.

It is ironic that Benmiller is now such a placid place, since this hamlet on Sharpe's Creek was a bustling mill community during the nineteenth century. Now all that remains is a complex of buildings snuggled into a narrow wooded valley — a quiet little world of its own. Peter Ivey remembered this sweet scene from childhood visits and was moved to purchase and renovate the historic buildings here as they became available. The result, the Benmiller Inn, is now in the hands of the International Order of Foresters, and is run by two capable and personable managers, Kathy Nichol and Randy Stoddart.

The Woollen Mill, a cast-lime knitting mill erected in 1877 to produce blankets, is the largest building. It is the heart of the inn, not only because it contains the reception desk, Jonathan's pub, and dining rooms, but also because it so thoroughly manifests the spirit of Benmiller. Great care was taken to retain the elements of the original building — rough, weathered timber, mill workings and tools — which have been meticulously restored. Barn boards have become doors, small gears have been turned into wall sconces, hand pumps have been wired to become lamp bases, industrial spools and bobbins have been worked into decorative screens, and hay forks have been transformed into mirror frames.

Each of the thirteen guest rooms in the Woollen Mill has a unique layout, with straw-plaster walls accented by barn-board trim. The rooms are individually furnished with antiques and recycled mill items. The beds are covered with handmade quilts, and all of the headboards, of wrought iron, are fashioned in the shape of the inn logo. The rooms have writing desks, and televisions are hidden in antique cabinets. As part of the inn's commitment to environmentally responsible management, the bathrooms are fitted with wall-mounted squeeze tubes for soap and shampoo. Some bathrooms are equipped with whirlpool tubs.

Gledhill House (1906), a gracious grey building with a black Mansard roof, was designed to follow the curves of the mill pond's bank. Originally a mill owner's house, it now has seventeen guest rooms and two spacious meeting rooms. All rooms have French doors leading onto a romantic patio or balcony that overlooks the pond. The view is beautiful in any season, but spectacular in fall when the brilliant foliage of the wooded slopes surrounding the pond are reflected in a watery mirror. The rooms are tastefully decorated with antiques and reproductions, but also with the same whimsical treatment as the mill. All of the rooms come with a small kitchenette, and some have a fireplace or a private sauna. Gledhill House has a radiant heating and cooling system that uses solar energy for winter heating and the cool waters of Sharpe's Creek for air conditioning.

The River Mill, a remarkable two-building complex, was transformed from a dilapidated grist mill covered with steel siding into an elegant building with oiled cedar siding on the exterior and exposed beams and rough straw plaster on the interior. The main portion of the building houses the exercise room, sauna, rooftop sundeck and magnificent indoor pool. Sharpe's Creek rushes over the dam into the Maitland River, and an enclosed walkway over the torrent connects the mill to fourteen guest rooms that have commanding views over the river.

The River Mill is decorated with recycled plumbing patterns rescued from a warehouse undergoing demolition. They were cleaned, polished and reused as accents, wall sconces, mirror frames, end tables and dresser-drawer handles. The calla lily design on the flour sacks found in the mill was silk-screened onto cotton and used for draperies and blinds. River Mill rooms have small kitchenettes, and the bathrooms are finished in colourful, hand-painted Mexican tiles.

The Mill House, especially secluded, has two deluxe suites and two rooms. The suites are like small apartments, with fireplaces, wide window seats with glorious views, and generous space for entertaining. The beds are covered with lamb's-wool duvets, and the couches and cushions are upholstered in chintz, in pastel colours. Pine furnishings are used throughout, including the armoire that hides the small kitchenette.

The rustic atmosphere of the Benmiller buildings
blends harmoniously with the pretty river valley,
which has been left in its natural state as much as
possible. Aside from Saturday-morning historic
tours and Sunday-afternoon guided nature walks,
there are few organized recreation programs at the inn:
the philosophy is to allow guests to enjoy the property in their
own way and at their own pace. There are several kilometres of
trails on site that provide very scenic hiking along the creek, past
two mill ponds and up the steep valley sides. The inn's trails link
up with those at the adjacent Falls Reserve Conservation Area to
provide a total length of over 20 kilometres. The conservation
area's river rapids make for a fun swim, and you can surf the
rapids or, for the less daring, bask in a small sun-warmed pool
among the rocks.

For guests who crave more activity, whether it be dogsledding, snowmobiling, windsurfing or sailing, the innkeepers can
connect you with equipment, instruction and guides. One doesn't
have to travel off site for fishing, of course, since
both Sharpe's Creek and the Maitland River are
productive trout streams, and the inn has several pairs
of hip waders for guest use.

Benmiller's wooded, watery setting is lovely in every season,
but it has a special appeal in the winter. The upper mill pond
freezes over to provide skating, and the hiking trails of summer
become groomed cross-country ski trails. The inn rents ski equipment, as well as snowshoes specially designed for the
steep slopes of the valley. The narrow topography
of the valley shelters the inn from winter winds, so
that snow stays balanced on tree branches and
shrubs, and presents a scene worthy of Currier and Ives.

Huron County is quiet family farm country. The innkeepers
can provide guests with maps of local byways, and guides to hiking, cycling, fishing and farm produce. They are also happy to put
together picnic baskets for daytrippers. Mountain bikes are available for rent to those who enjoy travel by pedal power.

The nearby town of Blyth has more than just a theatre festival. Blyth was initially a tannery town, and two leather outlets,
with a wide selection of leather, suede and sheepskin clothing for
men and women, remain.

Goderich, the county seat, is worth a day's visit. It has an
unusual octagonal town plan and street after shady street of grand

nineteenth-century mansions. The Huron County Pioneer Museum has exhibits, dioramas and films that describe various facets of local history. Some of the galleries are spacious enough to accommodate reconstructed train engines, windmills, and even entire street scenes. Another historic site — and one not to be missed — is the Huron Historic Gaol. An imposing structure of rough stone, it also has an octagonal plan, with walls 5 metres tall and almost 1 metre thick. Self-guided tours let you survey the 1842 rooftop courtroom, the dreary concrete cells, and the Edwardian comfort of the adjacent governor's house. Goderich prides itself on its waterfront, which has a beautiful white-sand beach and a boardwalk promenade. As any local will tell you, if you are quick you can see the sun set twice — once from the beach, and a second time from the nearby cliff.

Many guests prefer to stay in and soak up the peaceful, placid atmosphere at the inn. Premium pampering is available by way of spa services (massages, facials, manicures and the like), which can be arranged by appointment any weekday. You don't need to step off the site to find souvenirs, as the gift shop is well supplied with local pottery, handmade sweaters, gift cards, folk-art birdhouses, preserves and beeswax candles.

A day of rejuvenation, whether spent on the trails, on the waterfront, or curled up by fire, can be suitably capped off with the inn's "nouvelle cuisine with a rustic flair". The inn has done a good job of searching out local food stuffs so that their kitchen produces dishes that can't be found anywhere but here. (The staff are quick to point out that Huron County is Canada's highest producing agricultural county east of Winnipeg.) The dining room is very pleasant; Sharpe's Creek is an arm's length outside the windows, and the forest opposite is carpeted with daffodils in spring and ashimmer with gold foliage in autumn.

The chef is Derek Griffiths, a graduate of Humber College who received his practical training in this very kitchen. The Chambers Farm rabbit with a pommery mustard crust, and roast pork tenderloin with slivered pears and apple chutney are highly recommended. Lunch is just as appetizing as dinner, and choices include Blyth Acres rainbow trout wrapped with prosciutto en papillote, and Benmiller pizza topped with glazed onions, oyster mushrooms and a variety of cheeses. Finish off with a sun-dried-cherry brulée or honey crunch pecan tart and one of the inn's specialty coffees, and you'll be well sated indeed.

The Benmiller Inn is like a separate world of relaxation and contentment, the secluded natural setting and the rustic, historic atmosphere are maintained by dedicated innkeepers. It's a winning combination with timeless appeal.

Benmiller Inn

R.R. 4
Goderich, ON
N7A 3Y1
(519) 524-2191
1-800-265-1711
Fax: (519) 524-5150
Innkeepers: Kathy Nichol and Randy Stoddart

47 rooms
Dining room open to the public
Directions: From Highway 8 between Clinton and Goderich, turn onto Huron Road 1 at Benmiller sign.
Tariffs: moderate
On site: indoor pool, exercise room, sauna, hiking, cycling, fishing, cross-country skiing, skating
Off site: Blyth Festival, Huron County Festival, Huron County Pioneer Museum, Huron Historic Gaol, shopping, country drives, fishing, boating, beaches, sea kayaking

KETTLE CREEK INN

Port Stanley

The Kettle Creek Inn began as a private residence, in the 1840s, on land originally purchased by village-father Colonel Bostwick. The property changed hands several times and was opened as an inn during the middle part of this century. The building fell into a despicable state of ruin, but thanks to Jean and Gary Vedova, it has been fully rehabilitated and is now a busy hostelry and meeting centre. The architecture of the inn is unusual. The main inn has five guest rooms and two suites, and five more rooms and three luxurious suites are located in two separate multi-storey guest houses. The buildings — in grey and blue clapboard with white trim — are clustered around a private garden courtyard. The new buildings are a perfect match to the original in colour and architectural detail, and the scene resembles a small village.

Most rooms have queen-size beds, and many have day beds that double as sofas and extra sleeping space, a bonus for traveling families. The suites in the guest houses each have a bedroom, a separate living area with a fireplace, and a spacious bathroom with whirlpool and pedestal sink. The rooms and suites at the Kettle Creek Inn have a spare, uncluttered look, with muted colouring that creates a fresh, relaxing atmosphere.

Jean Vedova is an enthusiastic promoter of Elgin County artists, and each room at the Kettle Creek Inn features original paintings and prints by a different artist — usually local scenes. No other Ontario inn puts as much care into the selection of artwork for its private guest rooms. The Designer Suite was even decorated by an artist.

The heart and soul of the Kettle Creek Inn is its garden — a masterpiece of colour, texture, and fragrance. The secluded courtyard that connects the inn and the guest houses functions as an outdoor restaurant. At its centre is a grand white gazebo fashioned from columns and gable ends that were rescued from a house undergoing demolition in nearby London. The gazebo is a choice eating spot, as are the tables overlooking the water garden, the most verdant area of the courtyard. There is always a plant in peak bloom, from spring magnolias to fall asters, with lilies, roses and clematis in between. With careful nurturing, Japanese maples thrive in this protected location. The garden is so lush that the plants spill out of their beds and over the pathways.

The indoor dining room is crisply decorated. Bistro tables with blue tile surfaces are dressed up with white linens and fine china in the evening. Port Stanley is a working fishing village, and yellow perch and pickerel are the menu items of choice. The lunch menu includes perch burgers and the dinner menu offers perch fillets fried with lemon and parsley. (Guests may even have their own catch cooked to order.) Other fishy items include fish soup Provençal, steamed mussels, and marinated salmon with orange whiskey dressing. The kitchen has a decidedly Mediterranean leaning. Bruschetta, rustic Italian pizza (with red peppers, olives, fontina and authentic panchetta), and mezze penne rigate (grilled smoked chicken, with pesto, roasted peppers and romano cheese) are house specialties. A meal can be finished off with freshly prepared sweets from the dessert menu, which includes raspberry chocolate torte, blueberry pie and carrot cake.

The Kettle Creek Inn is gaining attention as a centre for small-business retreats. Small groups can book the entire inn and transform it into a private retreat. A fully equipped meeting room is available, and parlour and dining areas can be arranged as break-out rooms. The innkeepers can organize special outings for small groups, such as fishing or sailing charters, golf days or bird-watching expeditions.

The north shore of Lake Erie is getaway country. Uncrowded beaches, fishing villages, historic sites and an antique railway are just some of its delights. Next time you're struck with the urge for a maritime holiday, take a short jaunt to Ontario's own seaside, Erie Country. Quaint Port Stanley, on the lakeshore due south of London, is a convenient base for exploration, partly because of its location midway along the lake's north shore, and partly because of the Kettle Creek Inn, which has been home port to sailors and landlubbers alike for over a decade.

No matter what direction you take from Port Stanley, an interesting adventure awaits. Drive west along Highway 3 to Rondeau Provincial Park, beloved by naturalists as a precious remnant of the lush, viny Carolinian Forest that once covered Southwestern Ontario. Rondeau's six hundred plant species include southerners tulip tree, sassafras, and nineteen species of orchid. The forest is habitat to a correspondingly southern community of animals, among them prothonotary warblers, spiny soft-shelled turtles and fox snakes. Bald eagles nest each year in tall trees along the back-bay marshes. Rondeau's level topography makes for easy hiking and cycling, while its lake winds are ideal for windsurfing and its marsh canals are popular with canoeists. (Rentals are available from nearby private outfitters).

An enjoyable daytrip can also be taken eastward from Port Stanley. Drive north on Highway 4, turn east along County Road 27, and drive to tiny Sparta, which started out as a Quaker settlement but is now a hamlet serving daytrippers. Village merchants are happy to provide a guide to local sites of interest, among them a Quaker meeting house with separate entrances for men and women, a cobblestone house, and two adobe buildings. The village has several interesting shops and galleries, most notably the studio of painter Peter Robson. Although best known for his watercolours of Ontario landscapes and historic buildings, Robson is often commissioned to produce immense, highly symbolic murals, and fortunate visitors may find one of these works in progress in the studio.

Drive south from Sparta; then follow the succession of county roads that hug the lakeshore. The broad, breezy beach at Port Burwell Provincial Park is never crowded and churns up a good strong surf for aquatic play. Twelve kilometres east of Port Burwell is Sand Hill Park, one of the region's natural wonders. A sand bluff 135 metres in height, which owes its origin to the prevailing winds, has attracted tourists since the early 1800s. The hill (now a private campground that charges a modest entry fee) is a demanding climb, but the intrepid are rewarded with a unique lookout over restless Lake Erie.

Farther east along Lake Erie's shore is Port Dover, a town famous for yellow perch. Both a recreational fishery and a commercial fleet here are based on this sweetest of freshwater denizens. Even if you don't fish, the town is worth a visit. The Harbour Museum pays tribute to the lives of ordinary people who have gleaned a living from this treacherous inland sea. The exhibit includes tools used in modern fishing and items that have washed up on shore and been caught in fishing nets. It also has charts and text that describe famous Lake Erie wrecks. Port Dover also offers a beach, a large marina, some good seaside shops, and the Lighthouse Festival Theatre.

Port Stanley itself can be easily surveyed by foot, and many of its charming spots are within a block of the inn. The inn is located at the heart of the tourist shopping area, and many shops are housed in old fish warehouses and historic homes. The anchor of the street is the flagship store of the Kettle Creek Clothing Company, well known for its fashionable clothing in natural fabrics. Local merchants have put together a walking tour brochure that describes the history of downtown buildings.

It's just about impossible to walk from Kettle Creek Clothing to the harbour without stopping at Broderick's Ice Cream Parlour. Not only do they offer dozens of inviting flavours in warm-off-the-grill waffle cones, but they also specialize in extravagant concoctions, such as hot praline and summer-fruit sundaes. Once fueled up, continue downhill, past the Port Stanley Festival Theatre and across the King George Lift Bridge, to the Port Stanley Terminal Railway (est. 1856). The railway is a magnet to railroaders young and old. Disrepair once threatened the line, but railway enthusiasts came to the rescue and breathed new life into the London–Port Stanley. Trains now carry passengers on return trips to Union, White's Station, and the town of St. Thomas. The trains run all summer and on weekends during spring and fall, and special Santa Claus runs are held during December.

Port Stanley has several options for fun in the sun. There are two beaches, named Big Beach and Little Beach, and golf and tennis facilities nearby. Fishing charters are very popular, and there's even an annual salmon derby.

Just north of town is Moore Water Gardens. This nursery deals exclusively in the fragile and elegant water plants used to beautify waterfalls, fountains and ornamental ponds. The nursery ponds are lush with plants that always seem to be in radiant, spectacular bloom.

Seaside villages are great places for escape. Next time you are thinking about heading for the east coast for a Maritime holiday, save yourself considerable time and cash and take advantage of our own "seaside" — the fabulous Lake Erie shore — and the hospitality of the Kettle Creek Inn.

Kettle Creek Inn

216 Joseph Street
Port Stanley, ON
N5L 1C4
(519) 782-3388
Fax: (519) 782-4747
Innkeepers: Jean and Gary Vedova

15 rooms
Dining room open to the public
Directions: The inn is at the traffic lights in the centre of Port
    Stanley.
Tariffs: inexpensive
On site: ornamental gardens
Off site: Port Stanley Festival Theatre, Port Dover Harbour
    Museum, Moore Water Gardens, Rondeau Provincial Park,
    Port Stanley Terminal Railway, shopping, beaches, golf,
    tennis, fishing

WESTOVER INN

St. Marys

Westover Inn is a dignified grey-stone mansion surrounded by 8 hectares of lawn and garden and ancient old trees. The inn was built in 1867 as a home for William and Joseph Hutton, local businessmen who achieved financial success as owners of St. Marys Cement and numerous other enterprises. A red-brick dormitory wing was added when the home became a Roman Catholic seminary during the 1930s. Eventually the property was purchased and extensively refurbished to accommodate guests.

Guests may book rooms in three separate buildings. The original stone manor has five spacious, high-ceilinged rooms. Each of these has a large bed decked out in a floral spread and a coordinated bed skirt, a small sitting area, and a writing table. All rooms overlook the lush grounds, but the most romantic have stained-glass windows and private balconies. Few inns offer guests as private accommodation as Westover's modern Terrace. The Terrace has twelve contemporary guest rooms. The Cottage, the former dormitory for the seminary has several one-bedroom suites and living rooms, some of which have private patios.

The grounds at Westover have traditionally been maintained in a lawn-and-flowerbed state, but the current innkeepers are dedicated to a policy of composting, recycling and organic garden maintenance, and there is a small but ever-increasing wildflower meadow near the Cottage building.

Chef Michael Hoy has shaped the inn's menu around local ingredients, including garden-fresh vegetables and organically raised Perth County beef. Most lunch menus include soups, salads and sandwiches, but at Westover these dishes become something special through a selection of non-traditional ingredients. A salad, for example, may have shrimp and scallops with avocado, melon, cucumber and red onion. Choice of soup may include chilled young carrot and fennel, and a Westover sandwich may be filled with grilled eggplant, zucchini, pepper and tomato, and flavoured with goat cheese and red-pepper ketchup.

Dinner begins with crab and salmon cakes or a roasted pepper tart. Entrees include roast venison with sun-dried cherries, pearl onions and juniper. Save room for dessert: chocolate mayonnaise cake served on stewed rhubarb. The inn also makes its own breads and other baked goods, ice creams and sorbets. Westover Inn holds several food events. Each month, from October to April, a special dinner focuses on the cuisine and wines of a different country. France, Italy and Ireland are often featured. St. Patrick's Day is celebrated with a Celtic band, Guinness beer, and traditional Irish foods.

The dining room at Westover, once used as the seminary chapel, has the deep mouldings, high ceilings and floral fabrics of a grand old house. The neighbouring bar, with its black-and-white-tile floors and bistro tables, is perfect for live music and an après-theatre libation. During the warm months, the outdoor patio is the place to be. Bordered by daylilies and shaded by enormous maples, the patio overlooks the "garden mound," a shrine to Our Lady of Fatima. The postcard-pretty tea house, which the Hutton brothers had built for their mother, may be reserved for private dinner parties.

Westover Inn is within a short walk or drive of many of St. Marys' best attractions. Start off with a swim in the marvellous quarry, which is touted as Canada's largest natural outdoor swimming pool. Your hosts will be happy to arrange a choice tee time at any of the three good courses nearby, and tennis is available at municipal courts. The nearby Wildwood Conservation Area offers hiking, swimming and windsurfing during the summer, and ice fishing, tobogganing and cross-country skiing during the winter. Downhill inner tubing is great outdoor fun, and it can be enjoyed at the River Valley Golf Club.

Two long-distance hiking trails, the Thames Valley and the Avon, are both within easy access of the inn and run for many kilometres along the river in both directions. But you don't need to be a serious hiker to enjoy walking in St. Marys, for it is one of the best villages in Ontario for strolling. (Be sure to take along a copy of the local historical guide.) The town's glorious hills, a rarity on the Southwestern Ontario plains, are adorned with Victorian buildings — stone commercial blocks, an imposing Town Hall and Opera House, and dozens of beautifully preserved mansions built by wheat and cement magnates. The downtown even boasts the store where Timothy Eaton and his brothers first practiced as retailers.

St. Marys is a perfectly central location for daytrips and backroad rambles through the heart of Southwestern Ontario. The region has dozens of villages, yet no village is as amply endowed with antique vendors as Shakespeare, which makes it an ideal starting point. The hamlet is just east of Stratford, at the intersection of Highways 7/8 and 59. Jonny's Antiques, J. Donald Antiques, Kathleen's, Glen Manor and Land & Ross — all are veterans of the antique scene, and an exploration of these stores is sure to turn up something irresistible, whether a Victorian Chinois screen or a tortoise-shell business card holder. The Harry Ten Shilling Tea Room is not only a good place to take a very English tea or ploughman's lunch, but is also a source of imported English paintings and prints. At Chanticleer it's Christmastime all year round; this store has enough trees, garlands, nutcrackers and wreaths to keep you decking the halls for a decade.

Most visitors to the area take in a play at the Stratford Festival. Performances take place in three different theatres, and, along with Shakespeare's plays, the program includes classic and contemporary drama from Europe and North America as well as an annual musical extravaganza.

But Stratford has many other charms aside from the theatre. Lakeside picnics are popular, and take-out feasts can be arranged through Lindsay's Food Shop and the Festival Bakery and Café (both on Wellington Street), the festival theatre's own Greenroom, or the Boathouse River Patio (on York Street). The lovely Shakespeare Gardens lie between the striking dichromatic Perth County Court House (1887) and the river. When the town is bustling with sightseers, the gardens, which feature plants commonly grown in Shakespearean England — hyssop, yarrow, anise, pennyroyal, sweet woodruff — can be a tranquil retreat.

Although new shops commonly spring up along York and Ontario Streets, some old favourites include Gregory Connor Antiques, Props, Gallery 96 and Callan Books. Stratford also has excellent restaurants, among them Rundles (9 Cobourg Street), the Old Prune (151 Albert) and the Church (Waterloo Street).

St. Marys is also within striking distance of the fascinating oil boom towns of Petrolia and Oil Springs. Petrolia Discovery is a superb museum. Displays utilize an exemplary collection of historic documents and artifacts that, together with the NFB film

Hard Oil, paint a clear picture of Ontario's nineteenth-century oil industry, the evolution of Imperial Oil, and modern oil refining techniques. The museum is also home to a working oil field that produces a small but steady 225 barrels a month using nineteenth-century equipment. The guided tours, led by knowledgeable museum staff, are highly recommended.

Few Ontarians realize that the worldwide petroleum industry got its start right here, on the expansive prairie of Lambton County. Oilmen were drawn here for a boom that lasted from 1860 to 1900, although there are still hundreds of active wells in the area. Fabulous wealth was generated for a number of local magnates, and where wealth goes, interesting settlements also seem to crop up. On a stroll through tranquil Petrolia, note the streetlight standards modelled after oil rigs, and the Victorian Opera House, hospital and train station.

The story of petroleum geology and its importance to modern life is best researched at the Oil Museum of Canada, in Oil Springs. Among other things, you'll learn that the history of petroleum actually began about four hundred million years ago, when this region lay under a warm tropical sea. The remains of plants and animals were eventually compressed, resulting in oil beds. Fossil remains of this early life have been exposed through the strong erosive action of the Ausauble and Rock Glen Rivers, and the Rock Glen Conservation Area near Arkona is a wonderful place to spend a few hours fossil hunting. Park regulations stipulate that only one specimen of any kind of fossil may be removed, and that no digging is allowed. Nevertheless, success is pretty much guaranteed, and there is no more exciting souvenir to take home with you than a well-preserved little trilobite, coral or brachiopod.

Whether you spend your time exploring the depths of the Ausauble gorge, or the dark recesses of an antique store, you'll no doubt appreciate the restful atmosphere of the Westover Inn.

Westover Inn

300 Thomas Street
St. Marys, ON
N4X 1B1
(519) 284-2977
1-800-COTTAGE

Fax: (519) 284-4043

Innkeepers: Julie Docker, Stephen McCotter, and Sean (Reg) Jackson

22 rooms

Dining room open to the public

Directions: St. Marys is north of Highway 7, between Stratford and London. Westover is in the west end of town.

Tariffs: moderate

On site: swimming pool

Off site: Stratford Festival, Petrolia Discovery, Oil Museum of Canada shopping, antique hunting, fossil hunting, golf, hiking, swimming, windsurfing, cross-country skiing

5

ELM HURST INN

Ingersoll

The joy of touring the area around London is that you can enjoy the best of the city and the county in one holiday. You can spend part of your escape at a sophisticated city museum or at the theatre, and explore an unusual nature reserve and a few country attractions during the remainder of the holiday. The Elmhurst Inn, in Ingersoll, is conveniently situated for an exploration of the London area, and provides package getaways that take advantage of both the urban and the rural facets of the area.

Elm Hurst is a yellow-brick Victorian mansion. Its four-storey tower, elaborate gingerbreading, steep black roof, and Gothic lancet windows with ornate brick surrounds warm the souls of all lovers of heritage buildings. The home has a historical connection with the cheese industry. One of the founding fathers of cheese-making in Southwestern Ontario was James Harris, and this building was constructed as his home in 1872, about seven years after he established a cheese factory on the same property. In order to promote Ingersoll cheese, Harris coordinated the production of a mammoth cheese — 3.5 tonnes in weight and 6 metres in circumference — that was exhibited at the New York State Fair in 1866. Photographs of the huge cheese, loaded on its custom-designed cart (drawn by twelve horses) hang at the inn, and a historic plaque at the north end of the property provides more details.

In modern times, Elm Hurst was refurbished and opened as a restaurant, and after much success, was enlarged to provide space for guest rooms. The Elm Hurst dining rooms, in the oldest part of the inn, are replete with historic ambience. High ceilings with ornamental plaster work, deep baseboards and cornice mouldings, and original mantels present a picture of old-world elegance. The several small dining rooms with elegant table settings contribute to the refined atmosphere; there is even a private room that seats only two. (According to innkeeper Pat Davies, this romantic nook is a favourite spot for marriage proposals.)

Elm Hurst's Sunday brunch buffet is one of the finest in the province. Champagne and orange juice initiates the feast, followed by traditional breakfast fare such as eggs, pancakes, home fries, and made-to-order omelettes and waffles. A lavish spread of seafood, salads, cold meats and cheese serves as an appetizer. The centrepiece of the buffet is a carved roast sirloin, which is accompanied by another hot entrée such as spare ribs or roast chicken. The dessert table is amply laden with a wide selection of pies, mousse, cakes, and squares, although most people head straight for the inn's signature cherry trifle. The buffet is accompanied by live entertainment, usually a violinist or classical guitarist.

Dinners at Elm Hurst often have an international theme, and Asian, German, or Italian cuisine may be featured. In addition to the entrées are the chef's specialties, which include baked brie appetizer, prime rib and chicken fromage (suprême of chicken stuffed with herbed cream cheese and served with a Chardonnay dill sauce). The last Friday night of each month features a seafood buffet with unlimited portions of shellfish. The inn holds live entertainment on Friday and Saturday nights, and also hosts special events such as murder mystery weekends, wellness weekends (healthy foods, massage therapy, and fitness sessions) and comedy evenings.

The addition to the inn was designed so well that you would be hard pressed to determine where the old leaves off and the new begins. It encompasses the reception area and public rooms, which are decorated in rose, pink and deep green. There are numerous conference and meeting rooms, and a grand ballroom for weddings and other events.

The guest rooms are each slightly different in decor, and some are equipped with whirlpool tubs and fireplaces; executive suites have two rooms, a spacious living room and a separate bedroom. Several of the rooms have cathedral ceilings and immense windows that offer a terrific view over the creek and woods on the inn property.

The Elm Hurst is a strong supporter of local artists. Just behind the inn is a weathered barn (a re-creation of the Harris carriage house), which contains a large main-floor art gallery. The gallery features varied interpretations of the Elm Hurst Inn by Ontario artists Peter Robson, James Lumbers, Joyce Bridgett, Mary Farkas and Jan Cressman, among others. The adjacent gift shop sells homemade preserves, hand-knit goods, and a myriad of small crafts, as well as books about local history and culture. The lower floor of the carriage house has an exercise centre, and future plans include indoor and outdoor hot tubs, a massage room and a sauna.

The Elm Hurst Inn has 17 hectares of property upon which you can play volleyball, badminton, croquet and horseshoes. There is even a putting green for you to practice your stroke. The Inn has teamed up with the Thames Valley Conservation Authority to develop a 2.5-kilometre walking trail. During the summer, you might want to go for a short hike and enjoy a picnic lunch among the wildflowers. The "Hall's Creek Getaway" package includes accommodation, a box lunch, a trail guide and binoculars. Inn staff can also book you a choice tee time at the Ingersoll Golf and Country Club, arrange a horseback excursion at a local stable, or arrange a trip to Woodstock for harness racing.

Another popular Elm Hurst package, "Theatre Bound," includes accommodation, breakfast and tickets to a performance at the Stratford Festival, which runs from May to October. Just as the Stratford season winds up in the fall, the curtain rises at the Grand Theatre, in London, which hosts season after season of audience-pleasing hits, from drama to musicals to high comedy. Culture vultures will also want to visit the London Art Gallery, with changing displays of over two thousand works by Canadian and international artists.

London has several museums, the best known being Eldon House (1834), a Regency-Georgian white clapboard house that was home to four generations of the Harris family. Arranged to depict a typical Victorian household, Eldon House has an eclectic array of furnishings, including a grandfather clock, African hunting trophies, and a formal dining room set with fine china and silver. The grounds contain a period herb garden and offer an outstanding view over the Thames River.

On Wonderland Road, in the north end of London, lie the Museum of Indian Archaeology and the Lawson Pre-historic Indian Village. The archaeology museum holds tens of thousands of artifacts that, with the help of text, photographs and documents, depict early Native culture in Southwestern Ontario. The adjacent village is a reconstruction of a neutral Indian community that occupied this very site about five hundred years ago. Wooden palisades enclose several longhouses and garden plots.

The region between Ingersoll and Norwich has a wealth of intriguing nooks and crannies that are of great interest to naturalists and gardeners. Plan a visit to Sweaburg in late May, when the floral bloom at Trillium Woods Provincial Nature Preserve is at its peak. Here you'll see our provincial symbol in green, purple and even striped petals. (Please remember that picking trilliums is forbidden by law.) Map apple, jack-in-the-pulpit and foam flower are other spring beauties found at Trillium Woods.

Tiny Sweaburg has another site of interest, Jakeman's Maple Products, a family-run maple syrup operation located across the road from Trillium Woods. Pancake breakfasts, served from February to April, take place in a large hall filled with gingham-covered tables. Locals and tourists alike dig into mountains of pancakes, bacon and sausage in an atmosphere of country congeniality. Tours of the sugar bush are provided in season, and maple products are sold year round.

Gardeners from a wide area know McMillen's Iris Gardens near Norwich as the prime source of iris, Siberian iris and daylilies in Southern Ontario. Visit during the growing season (from June to August) and you'll witness vast growing fields in a tapestry of delicate sky blue and apricot, dramatic magenta and orange, and everything in between. Identify your favourites and place an order; the plants will be uprooted and shipped when the time is right.

Otterville, a tranquil village south of Norwich, is the home of The Herbal Touch, Marilyn Edmison-Driedger's herb business. Her shop is well stocked with dried herbs for decoration, wreaths, bouquets, homemade vinegars and oils and books. In her large but orderly herb garden, healthy plants burst forth with flower and strong perfume, and birds and bees busy themselves among the blooms.

Don't leave Otterville without seeing Treffey's Mill. This is one of the oldest continuously operating mills in Ontario, constructed in the mid-1800s. The municipal park here is a perfect picnic spot.

Ingersoll is a top producing region for milk and cheese. The story of local cheese manufacturing is told at the Cheese Factory Museum, which is situated at Centennial Park in central Ingersoll, (open from May to October). The museum is a board-and-batten re-creation of the simple cheese factories that were commonplace in the region about a century ago. Tools, machines, historic photographs, diagrams and a video illustrate the various steps in cheese making. Tavistock Cheese, in the nearby town of Tavistock, is the area's one remaining cheese plant. The outlet store sells dozens of kinds of cheese — Tavistock Cheddar is especially popular — at lower-than-retail prices.

Enjoy the best that city and rural life have to offer at Elm Hurst Inn, and be sure to take advantage of one of their package getaways.

Elm Hurst Inn

Highway 401 & 19
Ingersoll, ON
N5C 3K1
(519) 485-5321
1-800-561-5321
Fax: (519) 485-6579
Innkeeper: Pat Davies

49 rooms
Dining room open to public
Directions: Elm Hurst is located at the intersection of Highways 401 and 19.
Tariffs: inexpensive
On site: exercise room, skating rink, putting green, interpretive trail
Off site: London Art Gallery, Fanshawe Pioneer Village, Stratford Festival, harness racing, country drives, antique hunting, cycling, hiking, golf, cross-country skiing

LANGDON HALL

Cambridge

You are travelling, somewhat carefully, along a rutted country road that winds through a maple-beech forest and then climbs a short hill. The road curves left, the trees end abruptly, and the view is filled with a verdant sweep of lawn that leads the eye up to the the stunning majesty of Langdon Hall. Somewhat intimidated by its grandeur, you mount the stairs of the raised, two-storey portico toward massive black doors with round brass handles. Slowly the door opens to reveal, not a scene of stuffy formality, but an atmosphere so cheerful and relaxed that you are immediately convinced that you have come to the right place.

Langdon Hall is designed in the Colonial Revival style. The house is a picture-perfect ante-bellum mansion, except for its Ontario red-brick exterior. Langdon Hall is enormous — a 25,000-square-foot house with massive columns, a balustraded balcony and heavy front doors topped by an elliptical fanlight. A closer look reveals fine architectural details: modillion block cornices (square wooden mouldings under the eave), a roof accented with white, pedimented dormers, tall red chimneys and mullioned windows with shutters and ornamental keystones.

Langdon Hall has been the home of Langdon Wilks (a descendent of the Astors) and the infamous tycoon Hetty Green. About 90 hectares of land adjacent to Cruickston Park, the family summer home, was given to Wilks as a wedding present. A stay at Langdon Hall is to live in the spirit of America's golden era when landed gentry led a carefree, sporting life amid luxury and beauty.

Bill Bennett, an architect who was bitten with the innkeeping bug while designing the renovation of other unique country properties, and Mary Beaton, with a background in catering and an eye for decoration, were ideally suited to take on the formidable task of restoring Langdon Hall to its former glory. The main lobby and adjacent parlour are breathtaking rooms that have been ornately trimmed by master woodworkers. The walls are of solid-wood panelling, the doorways and fireplaces are flanked by columns and pilasters painted white, and the cornice moulding is done in Classical modillion block. The lobby features an atrium with ornate balustrades, where light pours in from above for an effect of cheery opulence. At the front desk, a squadron of uniformed, efficient staff members cheerfully see to every conceivable guest need, from shoe polishing to nightly turndowns.

Other public rooms include a ladies' parlour with a fireplace, a map room with an ancient billiard table, and a sunny lounge with deeply cushioned wicker furniture — just the spot for quiet conversation or a good read of the Sunday papers. All of these public rooms are furnished with antiques, many of which belonged to the Astor family. Portraits of family members hang in several rooms, a touch that adds to your sense of spending a week-end at a family estate. There are private nooks and crannies throughout the house, the most interesting being on the second floor beside the atrium, where an ancient card table and chairs sit ready for a game. The original Astor linen press stands nearby.

The home was renovated to accommodate eleven spacious rooms and two suites; some have a private balcony, and others have a two-storey layout with a main-floor living room and an upper-storey bedroom. The rooms are decorated with delicate pastel walls, white wood trim and chintz sofas. The inn's signature colour, a rich blue, is used for bedskirts, armchairs, lamps and other accents. Some rooms are supplied with wood-burning fire-places and fully equipped writing boxes, and the bathrooms come complete with terry robes adorned with Langdon Hall's crest. Each bed bears a lofty, white duvet embroidered with the same insignia, and a mountain of inviting pillows are propped up against a sleigh headboard modelled after Hetty Green's own. Many guests claim that these are the most comfortable beds they have ever slept on.

The Cloisters, a separate building with thirty guest rooms, is separated from the inn by perennial gardens but easily accessed either by a gravel pathway or an underground passage. The Cloisters is a Bill Bennett masterpiece, and few visitors perceive that it is actually a contemporary construc-tion. The building, built on top of the original garden wall, is aptly named, and as you walk the arcaded exte-rior corridor, you might expect a monk to appear around the cor-ner. The rooms here have the same high beds and white duvets as the main house, as well as fireplaces and generous sitting areas.

The bathrooms are luxuriously appointed with gleaming dark wood, deep soaking tubs and a full range of amenities. The double-door entry is a much-recommended European feature that provides greater privacy and quiet in the rooms.

The luxury continues, on the lower floor of the Cloisters, at Langdon's spa, which is fully equipped with a steam room, a sauna, a whirlpool, and an exercise room. Available treatments include aromatherapy massage, manicures and pedicures, herbal wraps, facials and body-glow polishing.

The dining room at Langdon Hall is elegantly simple, with white table linens over green cloths, hardwood floors, and chairs upholstered in striped fabric. The effect is to allow the colour and texture of the continental and country house dishes created by chef Louise Duhamel to come to the fore. Many of Duhamel's working materials are produced right on site. Vegetables come from the inn's garden, heritage apples from the orchard, honey from the apiary, and a springtime harvest of leeks, morels, violets and fiddleheads from the inn's own wildlands. The kitchen also makes its own baked goods, vinegars and preserves.

The meals served in the dining room are peerless. The dinner menu offers a lavish six courses, each of which presents a novel combination of taste and texture. You may start with goat cheese and cracked pepper wrapped in phyllo and served with an apple-cider dressing, or a warm salad with quail eggs and pine nuts. Memorable entrees include twice-cooked duckling with a raspberry, star anise and ginger sauce, and roasted veal and wilted greens with a sun-dried tomato, leek and potato gratin. Recommended grand finales include pumpkin crème brulée, and a luscious chocolate truffle cake. Your wines can be chosen from an extensive cellar that offers over a hundred choices and specializes in fine French products.

You could luxuriate in the sunny lounge after dinner, or sip a Cappuccino in the Wilks Bar (Langdon himself beams approval from the portrait over the hearth), but the magnificent grounds of the inn beckon. Dr. Leslie Laking, formerly head of the Royal Botanical Gardens in Burlington, meticulously researched period gardens, delineated the original flowerbeds, and attempted to replicate the gardens that were on the estate in Langdon's day. The perennials between the house and the Cloisters are particularly lovely, providing a rich tapestry of colour, shape, texture and fragrance.

There are more botanical delights beyond the Cloisters. Straight from a scene in *The Secret Garden*, these plantings are reached along a pathway that passes through several intriguing gates. The gates and walls were modelled after favourites discovered by Bennett and Beaton on a tour of colonial Virginia. The kitchen garden — as large as it is — is as straight-row orderly as a tiny patch. Here you'll find the cutting flowers, arugula, herbs and vegetables that appear on the evening table.

The expanse of manicured lawn near the garden is an official croquet facility, and, in order to preserve domestic harmony, the inn provides a booklet of official court layout and rules of play. Beyond the garden are a heated swimming pool, a tennis court and a change house that can double as a hospitality suite for corporate meetings. The grounds are the site of special events, including "Wind in the Woods," a series of Sunday-afternoon concerts held in June.

Langdon Hall's 90 hectares are covered in large part by mature Carolinian forest, which is normally found in the southern United States but is able to survive in this narrow region whose climate is moderated by Lake Erie. Carolinian species, which include the tuliptree, the cucumber tree and the sassafras, are increasingly uncommon species because the few remaining patches of forest are being lost to intensive agricultural and urban development. The forest's viny lushness is best appreciated from the inn's hiking and cross-country ski trails (a guide is available at the front desk).

There are few inns as ideally located for daytripping as Langdon Hall, and no one prepares her guests for a safari as well as Louise Duhamel. Her picnic baskets are filled with culinary treats, which may include goat-cheese stuffed chicken breast, poached salmon with a basil pesto crust, and strawberry tarts. A choice wine is tenderly tucked into the basket, alone with all of the necessary accoutrements — linens, cutlery and corkscrew.

The Grand River, recently designated a national heritage waterway, is coming into its own as a tourist resource. Canoeists are startled to discover that although the river winds its way through several cities, its valley remains wild and green, especially the prettiest stretch, between Cambridge and Paris. The innkeepers at Langdon offer a "Paddle to Paris" package, in conjunction with Canoeing on the Grand, to provide for a four-hour paddle, complete with a guidebook and shuttle service back to the inn. The river can also be enjoyed from the cycling trails that run along its banks. The inn has a few complimentary mountain bikes available for guest use, and can supply a map of routes. The Grand also has a reputation as the best fly-fishing waters in the province, and the innkeepers can connect guests with several local outfitters that supply guides and equipment.

Southwestern Ontario is renowned for theatre. Langdon Hall offers Stratford Festival packages that include accommodation, meals, and tickets for a play. Matinee fans are sent off with a picnic hamper, and those attending evening performances are served dinner on the terrace; post-theatre drinks and treats are served in the lounge. The Shaw Festival, in Niagara-on-the-Lake, another theatre of international calibre, is just an hour and a half away. Smaller regional theatres in Blyth, Drayton, and Fergus offer a range of home-grown and summer-stock plays at a small fraction of the cost of city theatres.

If you've ever had the feeling that you were born in the wrong era, and that you were really intended for the golden age of croquet tournaments and cucumber sandwiches, then head for Langdon Hall, the proud conservator of gracious living.

Langdon Hall

R.R. 33
Cambridge, ON
N3H 4R8
(519) 740-2100
1-800-268-1898
Fax: (519) 740-8161
Innkeepers: Bill Bennett & Mary Beaton

41 rooms, 2 suites
Dining room open to the public
Directions: Exit 275 on 401, take Fountain Street south, then
        Blair Road west through village of Blair to Langdon Road.
Tariffs: expensive

On site: spa, billiards, outdoor pool, tennis, croquet, hiking, cross-country skiing

Off site: Stratford Festival, Drayton Festival, Doon Heritage Crossroads, shopping, canoeing, fishing, cycling

JAKOBSTETTEL GUEST HOUSE

St. Jacobs

From the moment you see a farm with a "No Sunday Sale" sign at the laneway, fresh laundry billowing from the clothesline, and calico-clad women bending over long, straight rows of vegetables, you'll know that you are in a unique part of the province. The region north and west of Waterloo, settled by German-speaking Mennonites and Amish during the early 1800s, is one Ontario's most precious and vulnerable landscapes. St. Jacobs is the centre of the region, and a stay at the Jakobstettel Guest House is a perfect way to get the most out of a Waterloo County holiday.

Jakobstettel (pronounced Yakobstellel), located a couple of short blocks west of "downtown" St. Jacobs, is pleasantly removed from what can be a congested street scene on summer weekends. This grand Victorian red-brick house was built in 1898 for mill-owner William Snider, who was responsible for bringing hydro-electricity to the area. His father, E.W.B. Snider, lived in the palatial white house just across the street, and together these two homes bring to the neighbourhood an atmosphere of genteel elegance.

Jakobstettel has all the solid respectability of the Victorian era. An elegant wrought-iron fence and towering Norway spruce frame the view of the broad, curved porch and second-storey verandah with massive round pillars and rounded windows of leaded glass. Carpenters in the area have an excellent reputation for their craftsmanship, and the oak flooring on the main storey, in eye-catching inlaid mahogany and cherry patterns, demonstrates why. While the house may appear formal on the outside, the interior atmosphere is relaxed, with homey sofas and armchairs arranged around the fireplace in the parlour, and in the adjacent games room.

Visitors are reminded at every turn that they are in Waterloo County. Innkeeper Ella Brubacher, herself locally born and raised, has done a good job of creating a natural and appealing country atmosphere. In the games room, a crokinole board sits at the ready. Although now played worldwide, the game is indigenous to the region and has enthusiastic fans in many homes. The artwork in the house is also local, with historic photographs on the main floor and prints by Peter Etril Snyder and original oils by Evelyn Betz on the upper floors.

Jakobstettel has twelve guest rooms, each named after a town founding family, and framed histories of these characters hang on the walls inside the room. The focal point for each room is the bed, covered by a distinctive quilt designed and stitched by a local quilter. All of the quilts are lovely, but special mention must be made of the blue and white "Country Bride" quilt used on the four poster bed in the Snider Room; the gorgeous "Rose of Sharon" quilt in soft apple green, rose and white fabrics in the Smith room; and the dramatic brown and dark blue "Log Cabin" quilts in the twin-bedded Brubacher room. Curtains, wooden shutters, wallpaper, trim and mouldings are all coordinated to match the quilts. Most rooms have seating areas with armchairs or sofas, and several have access to quiet balconies. Many people request the main-floor suite, Doc Robinson's, in which the bedroom and adjacent living room face the grounds.

Guests take breakfast in a bright room off the kitchen. Freshly baked muffins, a fruit platter, various cheeses (including locally made Jersey Cheddar), granola and staff-made preserves are served buffet style. In this friendly setting, guests often while away an entire morning in conversation. No fear about the food running out — the 'stettel has an open-kitchen policy, so guests are welcome to open the fridge or investigate the cookie jar whenever the urge arises.

The inn's grounds are as lovely as the house. There are 2 hectares of lawn and gardens, with a swimming pool, a tennis court, a horseshoe pitch and volleyball and badminton nets. The garden gazebo is a preferred meeting room for the many corporate retreats and seminars that take place at Jakobstettel. Ella Brubacher provides such a relaxed and comfortable setting that many guests are content to spend their time sitting and appreciating the country peace and quiet.

For those guests who enjoy more active pursuits, the innkeeper has plenty of useful suggestions. The rolling countryside of the region is very photogenic, with wide river valleys, tiny hamlets with old-fashioned general stores and bakeries, and tidy Old Order Mennonite and Amish farms. With Ella Brubacher's recommended custom cycling tour (9 kilometres of traffic-free byways), and the single or tandem bikes available for guest use, you can travel through the countryside without disturbing the peace of this quiet community.

Brubacher can also help you arrange a horseback adventure at the Martin Farm, run by equestrian Barb Burechails. Her comfortable Tennessee Walking Horses are even tempered, so she can accommodate riders of many skill levels. The rides take visitors into the heart of the country, along the Conestogo River. There's nothing like riding through a herd of cows and fording the shallow waters to make you feel like an authentic cowpoke. Burechails offers half-day, full-day and overnight rides, and meals can be provided on the trail, although she will be pleased to tailor an outing to your needs.

Jakobstettel is conveniently located just metres away from the region's most pleasant walk, a 2-kilometre trail along Ontario's longest millrace. The path is sheltered and pleasant in any weather — productive for bird-watching — and ends at a dam where local children fish. During the winter, the ice on the millrace is cleared for excellent skating. The trail is heavily travelled, which means that the snow becomes packed down. This is good for walking, but not so great for cross-country skiing, which is better enjoyed at the Sand Hills Conservation Area near Elmira, a hilly pine plantation with many kilometres of trails.

In a few short years, St. Jacobs has been transformed from a rural backwater into a bustling tourist village. While at first glance the town is a mosaic of country craft shops, a closer inspection reveals studios and galleries that rank with the best in Ontario. At the south end of town is the Historic Bowman Weavery, where, for over sixty years, fabric scraps have been turned into multi-coloured rag rugs. Roger Witmer has a studio and gallery on the main street; his paintings portray rural life and historic homes.

Quilt making is one of the great traditions of Waterloo County, and Ruffled Elegance, which has a kaleidoscopic supply of fabric and notions and a full range of ready-made quilts, is St. Jacob's best-loved quilt shop. At the Forge and Anvil, blacksmiths fashion decorator items such as wall hangings, candle holders and fireplace utensils, as well as exquisite knives for the kitchen and the tackle box. In the same building, you can watch a corn broom being made at the Hamel Broom Company.

The greatest concentration of galleries at St. Jacobs is in the silos and adjacent sheds at the north end of the main street. In the silos are three St. Jacobs mainstays: Conestoga River Pottery, the Silo Weavers, and The Top Drawer. Glass artists work in front of the roaring furnace at the Thorn Glass Studio, creating delicate vases, bowls and platters etched with geometric patterns. Across the street is Artefacts Architectural Antiques, a treasure-trove for decorators. Several rooms here are filled with architectural detailing — columns, gable ends, floor grates, doors, mortise locks, gargoyles — all rescued from buildings undergoing demolition.

Next to quilts, Waterloo County is known for its baked goods, and the Stone Crock Bakery has an aromatic selection. Many patrons head straight for the "Long John" doughnuts and "morning glory" muffins. Another local tradition, shoo fly pie — heavily flavoured with dark molasses — is an acquired taste.

No trip to Waterloo County would be complete without a thorough tour of The Meeting Place, a small museum located next to the Stone Crock Bakery. Photographs, maps, text and a 20-minute video explain the religious beliefs and history of the Mennonites. The Meeting Place will also inform you of the rules of appropriate tourist etiquette while in the area, which include no taking pictures of our Old Order friends.

Although St. Jacobs has become one of Ontario's major shopping attractions, even its shops are eclipsed in popularity by the farmers markets located a 5-minute drive south of town. There are two huge markets, one on either side of Weber Street. The markets are open Thursdays and Saturdays year round and Tuesdays and Wednesdays during the summer. Both markets have scores of fruit and vegetable stands outside, and stalls with cheese, meats and sausage, handcrafts and preserves inside. At the Stockyards, you can watch a livestock auction and wander the narrow catwalks above the holding pens.

Because Jakobstettel is a bed and breakfast, you'll need to plan on dinner out. In St. Jacobs are Benjamin's Inn, which has an internationally inspired menu, and the Stone Crock Restaurant, where country-style ribs, chicken and farmer's sausage are served family style. Two restaurants in the community of Three Bridges serve Sunday buffet brunches. Riverside Maples, which features the foods of Eastern Europe, is a good place for a family gathering. The Three Bridges Restaurant has a bright and cheery room overlooking the Conestogo River and an ample buffet.

Waterloo County's simple rural appeal makes for a very

relaxed getaway. The reward for planning your country respite at Jakobstettel Guest House is that you get to stay in St. Jacobs, the heart of this pastoral district.

Jakobstettel Guest House

16 Isabella Street
St. Jacobs, ON
N0B 2N0
(519) 664-2208
Fax: (519) 664-1326
Innkeeper: Ella Brubacher

12 rooms
Bed and breakfast only
Directions: Jakobstettel is in St. Jacobs, two blocks west of the
    downtown.
Tariffs: moderate
On site: gardens, outdoor pool, tennis court
Off site: The Meeting Place, St. Jacobs Schoolhouse Theatre,
    shopping, farmers markets, fishing, golf, cycling, walking,
    horseback riding, cross-country skiing

THE ELORA MILL INN

Elora

The Elora Mill Inn is one of those rare, organic places that seems to grow naturally out of its locale, a virtue attributable not just to the way its massive limestone walls rise straight up from the rocky brink of the Elora Gorge, but also to the way the local landscape and social history work together to culminate in a fine inn. The Elora Mill is well prepared to provide guests with a variety-filled escape that combines outdoor adventure, cultural events and fine regional cuisine.

The Grand River is the raison d'être for the village of Elora, since it was the potential for harnessing its water power that first attracted the attention of entrepreneurs and settlers during the early 1800s. The present stone mill was built in 1859 on the site of an earlier wooden mill that was destroyed by fire. An enormous undertaking — its walls are 1.5 metres thick at the base and the building is over 30 metres tall — the mill was constructed within a few months by Scots stone masons. Their legendary skill provided the whole region with an enviable heritage of stone houses, stores, churches and factories. The mill is crafted in the same buff-coloured limestone as the cliff on which it stands, and its size appears all the more impressive by its perch beside the falls, where the Grand River churns and roars its way into a 30-metre deep, 2-kilometre-long chasm.

The mill was in active use until the 1970s, when it was purchased and renovated as an inn. Although the original millstones lie at the property's entrance and mill equipment decorates the Penstock Lounge, the renovation process was a merging of the old and the new. The Elora Mill is front and centre in a renaissance that is leading the village back to its river origins and towards greater self-sufficiency. The mill is back in operation, producing 150 kW of hydroelectricity; two thirds of this is used to power the inn's operations, and the remainder is sold to the village.

The inn has thrity-two rooms, including ten suites. The thick walls of the inn provide for deep window sills that become sunny nooks perfect for viewing the spectacular river gorge. The rooms have a simple, uncluttered look, with country quilts on the beds, a soothing colour scheme of deep blues and greens, and armoires created especially for the inn to hide modern intrusions such as televisions. Some rooms have four-poster beds, vaulted ceilings and kitchenettes. All bathrooms have unique soap dishes and sinks fashioned by local potter Geoffrey Stevens.

Guest rooms are also located in three nearby buildings — the John Ross House (a pretty red-brick cottage that was Elora's first post office), the Granary (an old livery stable and warehouse), and the Mill Cottage. Many of these rooms are private suites with loft bedrooms and fireplaces. The balcony and deck at the Mill Cottage are right on the water, making it a romantic honeymoon possibility.

The decoration of the lounge and dining room is a piece of brilliance. The rugged soul of the mill, exemplified by its limestone walls and massive beams, is enhanced by carefully chosen rustic accents — copper utensils, a basket of dried hydrangea, a mill-belt wheel recycled as a coffee table. The lounge has a view down the cedar rim that runs the length of the gorge's water-sculpted cliffs. In the midst of the torrential waterfall just outside the window, a tiny islet, known as the "Tooth of Time," defies both gravity and the force of water. The best view of the river is from the lounge's outdoor patio, which is refreshingly cool all summer. Winter guests prefer the comfort of the fieldstone fireplace that dominates the room.

The Mill Restaurant is committed to providing a dining experience that reflects the heritage of the mill and the region's founding peoples. Brian Holden, a master of regional country cuisine, uses locally produced foodstuffs to express that philosophy. It is Holden's task to express that heritage in his cuisine. Spring Valley trout, Wellesley apple butter, Woolwich Dairy goat cheese, Stoney Creek Dairy ice cream, and Gerrie Farm produce are just a few of the delights that are delivered to the kitchen each week. Holden turns these items into dishes unique to the Elora Mill, such as trout sausage (trout stuffed with mushrooms, onions, leeks and radicchio, and served with tomato sauce) and pork Wellesley (tenderloin stuffed with savoury dressing and apple butter, and glazed with apple-cider and honey). A highly recommended dessert is the supremely sweet maple, pecan and beer tart: eggs, pecans, sugar and maple syrup are cooked with Elora Pale Ale and served in a flaky pastry shell.

Dinners at the Elora Mill are often the basis for special events. Five nights a year a guest chef prepares and presents a tantalizing meal. One of the most popular nights in this "Chef's Night Out" series is led by Bertha Skye of the Six Nations Reserve, and is dedicated to Native cuisine.

The inn's cellar offers more Canadian wines than any other dining room in the province and has won the Ontario Cuvée award. The inn has a standard mark up for all its wines, which means that high-end wines are a good buy. The innkeeper is responsible for blending the Stoney Ridge wines that bear the Innkeeper's Reserve label of the Independent Innkeepers of Ontario, and for the wines that carry the Elora Mill Inn's own label.

A tasty granola made with oats, bran, wheat germ, nuts and dried blueberries energizes guests for an adventurous day. Guests can choose from a "basket of activities," and the inn draws on community resources to put together well-planned, revitalizing daytrips. The Grand River is paramount in these schemes. Whitewater kayaking and canoeing lessons and trips are provided through the experts at Equinox Adventures. A Grand Adventure is the name given a day-long conducted tour of the river between Elora and the covered bridge at West Montrose, 15 kilometres downstream. Guests may choose their mode of transport — by foot along the gorge trails, by paddle with expert canoeists, or by pedal along country backroads. Fly-fishing lessons, equipment and guiding are provided by the enthusiasts at Grand River Troutfitters; success is not guaranteed, but a good day is! For something completely different, get a view of the park and the gorge from the clouds during a two-hour sunrise or sunset hot-air balloon tour — another one of the inn's adventuresome outings.

Independent explorers will want to head for the Elora Gorge Conservation Area; the entrance to the park is a short drive from the inn. The park has many kilometres of hiking trails (one of which leads to "Hole in the Rock," a cavern even Tom Sawyer would be impressed with), sports fields, a swimming pond, and, in winter, cross-country ski trails. Just outside the park entrance are vendors who rent inner tubes for a leisurely float down the Grand.

Elora has a long history of musical excellence, and as good corporate citizens, the Elora Mill lends its enthusiastic support to the

Elora Music Festival, a three-week musical feast held every summer. Singers and musicians of national and international repute perform in a variety of spectacular venues. Ontario offers no greater pleasure than an evening concert in the Elora Quarry. Performers are on a floating stage, and the music reverberates off the rock to the enchanted audience sitting along the rim of the cliffs.

There are plenty of good vibrations at the inn itself. The Elora Inn Fireside Jazz series runs on eleven weekends between November and April, and brings top-calibre players — Hagood Hardy among them — to the inn for dinner shows on Friday and lounge performances on Saturday afternoon (all proceeds go to the Elora Music Festival). The inn's Christmas Festival is held early in December. The village is dressed up for the season, with twinkling lights and garlands, and choristers and pipers entertain diners as they feast on six courses of traditional holiday foods.

Theatre buffs can take advantage of the mill's proximity to the Grand Theatre in Fergus to combine a good meal with a play. Musicals, comedies and mysteries are performed all summer long by professional troupes. The comfortable theatre seems perfect as it is, but there are plans to expand the lounge facilities and introduce a theatre-instruction program. Theatre tickets may be purchased as part of an Elora Mill package.

Business groups patronize the Elora Mill for its superior meeting facilities, and to take advantage of its leadership effectiveness courses. The largest meeting room, Drimmie Hall, like the rest of the inn, has the rustic charm of coarse stone walls. Those stone walls are combined with striking stained-glass panels in the Tea Room, a smaller meeting room that is also popular for weddings. Smaller meetings are held in the John Ross House, which also makes an effective hospitality suite.

The Elora Mill has teamed up with Heroic Hearts Inc. to create single- and multi-day programs for corporate groups. Much of the program takes place high above the river, upstream from the mill, on the mill's own rope course. Some courses also include a rock climbing component; but don't worry, you're in good hands — the president of Heroic Hearts is Mount Everest climber Jim Elzinga.

Elora was already a tourist shopping village before the turn of the century. Many of its best shops are housed in picturesque stone buildings that back onto the river. Time-tested shops that should be on the agenda of any serious shopper include Cobwebs, for kitchenware and gourmet foods; the Elora Pottery, for work by Geoffrey Stevens; Pepe and Maureen's, for dazzling gold and silver jewellery; and Macleod's Scottish Shop, for tartans and highland sweaters.

The Elora Mill is the product of the blending of a diversity of elements — a heritage river, a historic inn, a love of music, and fine dining. It's a tried and true recipe and, like many travellers, you'll be asking for seconds.

The Elora Mill Inn

77 Mill Street West
Elora, ON
N0B 1S0
(519) 846-5356
Fax: (519) 846-9180

22 rooms, 10 suites
Dining room open to public
Directions: Elora Mill Inn is at the end of Mill Street in Elora, the main shopping street along the river.
Tariffs: moderate
On site: lounge
Off site: Wellington County Museum, Elora Music Festival, Fergus Highland Games, Fergus Market, shopping, kayaking, inner-tube rafting, hot-air ballooning, fishing, golf, hiking, swimming, cross-country skiing

BEILD HOUSE COUNTRY INN

Collingwood

Collingwood has been Ontario's four-season recreation area for decades, with excellent conditions for downhill skiing, canoeing, hiking and windsurfing. Collingwood's appeal has been sweetened by the The Beild House Inn, with its heavenly mix of gustatory delights, fanciful decor and well-organized day outings.

Although Beild House is located in the heart of Collingwood, a step across the threshold of this large red-brick home transports you into a true country inn. Innkeeper Stephanie Barclay's long career in fabric and design has paid off handsomely, as every inch of the 7,400-square-foot home has been orchestrated to produce a familiar, cozy atmosphere. Soft floral sofas are arranged around back-to-back fireplaces in the main living room, which has a fine library of books on Ontario's history and natural beauty. Other common rooms include the dining area, a lounge with a well-stocked refrigerator, and a basement room with a brick fireplace, a television and a VCR.

Beild House began as the 1909 home of Dr. Joseph Arthur. Arthur's main-floor offices now act as a two-bedroom suite perfect for two couples or a traveling family. The suite is furnished in antiques, and decorated in rose, green and floral prints. Like all the accommodation at the Beild House, the suite has Stephanie Barclay's signature style, with a very romantic bed complete with a canopy overhead and a surfeit of luxuriously plump pillows.

Few Ontario inns can boast as lavish, imaginative treatment in each guest room as the Beild. There's the royal-blue-and-tartan Windsor room, named after the Duke and Duchess of Windsor, in which some of the furnishings have regal connections: the bed actually belonged to the Duke and Duchess of Windsor, and the train schedule that adorns one wall dates to an 1864 royal tour of Canada. You'll lose your head over the Marie Antoinette room; all of the furnishings — picture frames, mirrors, footstools, tables and chairs — are gilded. The ornate candleholders were brought to Canada from France in 1850 by innkeeper Stephanie Barclay's grandmother. Stephanie's pièce de résistance is the dream-like Sultan's Tent, a glorious room complete with corner wood-burning fireplace, king-size bed tented in lace, and accents of exotic locales. The third floor of the inn has a couple of large suites, each with fireplace and romantic Juliette balcony. These rooms, recently added, are wonderful places to rejuvenate after a day on the slopes or trails.

Just as Stephanie Barclay brought a family history in art and fabric to her role as innkeeper, her husband, Bill, brought with him a family tradition in food — he is a descendant of the Christie cookie family. A typical weekend menu is based on his philosophy that Friday night is the time to unwind and relax and Saturday is the time for fine dining. Friday's dinner is a buffet of Greek and tossed salads, shepherd's pie, lasagna, sweet chicken curry, rice pilaf and chili. Mother may have made these soothing dishes as well, but not with the same flair; for example, the lasagna is made with homemade crepes, not noodles; the chili is properly prepared with chocolate; and the plum chutney is made from the Beild's own plums. During the summer, Friday night's welcome barbecue is just as informal, with chicken, ribs, sausage, potato and chick pea salads, and devilled eggs.

Saturday night is the time to dress up a little for a romantic five-course dinner. The grand affair actually begins late afternoon in the drawing room, with a traditional English tea (the Beild House has over twenty-three varieties of tea) and freshly prepared sweets. Hors d'oeuvres are served at half past six, and dinner is served at seven. This is Bill's finest hour, and he capitalizes on such fine local ingredients as white asparagus, salmon (smoked and fresh), trout, apples, pears, sausage and duck. The first course may be a warm duck salad with orange poppyseed dressing, or sautéed trout on spinach, with Mornay sauce and toasted almonds. Sorbet is served between courses. Pork tenderloin with rhubarb sauce and apple stuffing, lamb Genghis Khan, and, everyone's favourite, fresh herbed salmon in filo pastry, with tarragon mayonnaise, complete the main offering. Desserts, including drunken plum cake, dacquoise cake and strawberry broyage torte, are followed with gourmet coffee or tea and shortbread. The Beild House is not licensed, but Bill Barclay ensures that the local liquor store has a good selection of wines to complement the meals.

The Beild House breakfast is the best way to prepare for an active day. Guests choose from a dozen entrees (from eggs Benedict with smoked salmon to crêpes filled with Granny Smith apples and hazelnuts and topped with maple syrup and whipped cream), loads of fresh fruit, homemade jams and marmalades, and fresh-from-the-oven croissants, applesauce cake and muffins.

Only the Collingwood area, with its fabulous range of outdoor activities, could coax guests away from the table (although some packages include a picnic lunch.) During the winter, Ontario's best downhill skiing is a short drive away, and Bill, an expert skier, is happy to provide information on the best runs. There are also cross-country ski trails nearby. Summertime is golf time, and Beild staff can arrange choice tee times at several private local clubs and at the championship Monterra course at Blue Mountain. Other summer activities include windsurfing at Craigleith Provincial Park, spelunking in the Scenic Caves and Caverns, and plummeting the water slides and slide ride at Blue Mountain. Cycling is a popular activity, and you can test your legs on the steep hills of the escarpment, or meander along the level gravel bikeway that runs from Collingwood to Meaford.

The Barclay's goal is to have every guest participate in their dream activity — whether it's rock climbing or landscape painting. To that end, they have done a remarkable job of linking their guests with local expert guides. Ray Mueller, of the Cantour company, is a knowledgeable outdoorsman who takes Beild guests on half- and full-day canoe trips on local rivers and through the Minessing Swamp. The trips can be tailored for any skill level, and include snacks or lunch. Mueller also conducts nature hikes on the Bruce Trail that combine fresh air, exercise, and great vistas with talks on ecology, geology and botany. The Niagara Escarpment's magical combination of towering cliffs, lush ferns and brilliant fall foliage provides plenty of material for shutterbugs, and Mueller offers photography weekends. The wintertime is equally picturesque, and Mueller leads snowshoeing expeditions along a sheltered valley of the Pretty River. Perhaps the most exhilarating offering from Cantour's menu of adventures is dogsledding; imagine captaining your own sled and two-dog team at top speed through woods and meadow.

For those who crave a more relaxing weekend, the Beild has plenty of ideas for quieter pursuits. Collingwood is a treasure trove of historic architecture, and Bill Barclay gives guests a walking-tour brochure that describes the design and history of local buildings. He also conducts Friday-evening slide tours of the town's historic delights during the fall. At the Collingwood Museum, Great Lakes history buffs can relive the days when this town was an important port and ship-building centre. Stephanie Barclay can help you plan a day on the back roads, with advice on the best antique stores and art galleries. You'll love to pick through Clerkson's ever-changing offerings of antiques and decorator accents, and any shopper can fill a day with a trip to the tiny village of Creemore, a village about half an hour south of Collingwood.

The Beild House has added a spa to its list of offerings, located on the main street of Collingwood. You can go out just to be pampered, and return to the inn relaxed and revitalized at the end of the day. Spa treatments include massage, facials, manicures, pedicures and hairstyling.

Two premier historic sites in the region are must-sees, and can be visited in a single daytrip to the Midland-Penetanguishene vicinity. In Midland, Sainte-Marie among the Hurons is a recon-structed Jesuit mission that is built on its original site. The village, Ontario's oldest European settlement, functioned as a respite to itinerant Jesuits, and its society was a composite of Huron and French cultures. After an excellent introductory film, visitors enter the village, wherethe daily life of the Jesuits and Native Christian converts comes to life; basket-weaving, canoe construction, cook-ing, and other activities are demonstrated, and visitors may try their hand. There are summer-afternoon outings in replicas of the huge freighter canoes used by the Jesuits, and evening candlelight tours. The Naval and Military Establishment at Penetanguishene is also a delight. Penetanguishene dates to the early nineteenth cen-tury, when it began as a British naval town. Costumed guides describe the daily grind for officers, enlisted men, the town doc-tor, the cartographer, and others. A highlight is the afternoon and evening sails aboard two replica schooners, during which you trade salt-dog insults with the crew and are ordered to take a hand in working the sails and oars and swabbing the decks.

Even the younger members of the family will enjoy a Beild House escape. Several experienced babysitters on staff take chil-dren skating, swimming, to the library or to Y programs when parents need some private time. The little ones return to a private dinner of their own, allowing parents to fully enjoy a quiet repast.

The Beild House has many packages to offer guests, including romance packages, photography weekends, cycling packages, spa packages, "Secrets Revealed" cooking weekends, and photography weekends. With wonderful food, luxurious surroundings, and a full program of off-site activities, a Beild House stay is frequently given as a reward to deserving employees. Reward yourself — and a loved one — with a trip to the Beild House.

Beild House Country Inn

64 Third Street
Collingwood, ON
L9Y 1K5
(705) 444-1522
Fax: (705) 444-2394
Innkeepers: Bill & Stephanie Barclay

15 rooms
Dining room not open to public
Not licensed, but you are welcome to bring your own wine
Directions: Take Highway 26 to Collingwood. Beild House is two
    blocks south of the bay, one block west of downtown.
Tariffs: inexpensive
On site: games room
Off site: Beild House Spa (downtown), Collingwood Historic
    Museum, Martyr's Shrine, Sainte-Marie among the Hurons,
    Naval and Military Establishment, shopping, antique
    hunting, hiking, fishing, boating, beaches, horseback riding,
    canoeing, windsurfing, downhill and cross-country skiing,
    dogsledding, ice fishing

THE MILLCROFT INN

Alton

The incomparable Millcroft Inn is like the grapes that flourish in Southern Ontario's wine country: a perfect marriage of hardy Canadian rootstock and cultivated European vines. And just as our vineyards need time to produce praiseworthy vintages, the Millcroft has achieved its honour as Ontario's inn of renown through patient cultivation of guest services, property and cuisine. This is especially true of the inn's operation since it came under the care of innkeeper Wolfgang Stichnothe, whose expert attentions have raised a very good inn to the level of perfection.

The Millcroft began with a unique historic property — an 1881 knitting mill of ochre stone, with cinnamon-coloured stone lintels over mullioned windows. The setting of this handsome, substantial building is made especially spectacular by its location on the Credit River. Water streams in a white veil over the mill dam; above the dam lies the flat, reflective waters of the mill pond, and below, the river tumbles over logs and rocks. The inn's property includes 45 hectares of meadow and wooded hills, which protect the inn from outside intrusion.

The historic appeal of the mill has been preserved in the interior as well, where irregular stone walls and exposed beams are visible in the public rooms. A central atrium brings a flood of natural light into the centre of the building. Flagstone and brick flooring, fires glowing in stone hearths, and antique accents — such as the two refinished carousel horses at the reception desk — complete a picture of luxury on the pioneer frontier.

The Millcroft Inn has fifty-two guest rooms in two heritage buildings and modern crofts. It is one of those rare inns where all guest quarters are equally desirable. The mill proper has twenty-two rooms, each individually decorated with Canadian and European antiques picked from local shops and sales. Handsome coffee-table books sit ready for your perusal in ample seating areas furnished with sofas, armchairs, and elegant writing desks. The most sought-after room in the inn occupies the upper storey of the glass pod that is cantilevered over the river; fortunate occupants book this room well in advance.

Twenty croft units are located on the opposite side of the river from the mill, a short walk across a bridge that offers an attractive view of the river. The two-storey crofts are much like townhouse cottages, with grey exterior siding and private entrances. The layout consists of a main-floor living room and bathroom, and a loft bedroom. The newly refurbished decor is bright and upbeat, with white walls, colourful fabrics, and a fireplace decorated in copper or ceramic tiling. Each living room has two couches that can be made into single beds, and a walkout to a private deck. Two of the crofts have private outdoor hot tubs sheltered by a white cedar forest: the perfect après-ski spot.

The crofts form a central quadrangle with a patio, pool and hot tub; bar service and snacks are available on the patio during the high season. The Mill's games room — with table tennis, billiards, darts and card tables — and fully equipped exercise room are also located in the croft area.

The Millcroft also offers ten rooms in the renovated Manor House, which was originally the mill owner's house. The interior appointments include antique furnishings and heritage colours. Manor House rooms are very spacious, with comfortable seating areas and writing desks; many bathrooms have double whirlpool tubs, and one has an antique claw-footed tub. The Manor House faces a lovely bi-level garden where a white arbour, a fountain and lush flowerbeds provide a romantic backdrop for weddings and other special events. Future plans include restoring the gardens to their nineteenth-century appearance.

Pleasant, well-appointed rooms are only the beginning of a blissful visit to the Millcroft Inn. It is the kitchen — with its consistency in excellent preparation and inventive presentation — that has left the name Millcroft on the lips of so many happy patrons, and put it high on the preferred list of every conference planner in Central Ontario. The Millcroft takes local trout, venison, and garden produce, and, with continental flair, produces a truly successful taste experience. Chef Reinhard Scheer-Hennings prepares wonderful menus, making full use of the inn's own pastry and baking team.

Favourite first courses include a generous portion of scallop seviche served in a crisp phyllo ring with truffle julienne, mustard oil and red-pepper juice. Fans of coarse-textured country pâté will love the Millcroft version of venison and buffalo served with Cumberland sauce and a Waldorf or cabbage salad. The dinner menu offers a dazzling diversity of tastes, from grilled breast of Muscovy duck in an anise and green peppercorn sauce and served with wild rice, lingonberries and a vegetable bouquetière, to a seafood pot-au-feu with tiger shrimp, scallops, mussels and salmon, in a fennel lobster broth with Pernod. For lunch I recommend the Caledon rainbow trout, which is perfectly sautéed and served with leeks, lemon and caraway.

The Millcroft's pastry chefs deserve special mention. In a house with such superlative main dishes, some of the inn's most sought-after foods are its finishing touches. Few diners ever forget the signature meringue swan glacé, a melt-in-your-mouth swan filled with ice cream and served with a wild raspberry coulis. Which brings us to the homemade ice creams; they are available in several flavours, including traditional Belgian chocolate and innovative and tongue-tingling anise and fig.

At breakfast, humble foods are elevated to something special. Porridge is served with vanilla custard sauce, cream and fresh fruit (the three bears would not have left this on the table!), and omelettes are filled with avocado, baby shrimp and tomato and accompanied by apple ginger compôte and rösti potatoes. These fine meals are served in the dining room that overlooks the river (the choice tables in the glass pod must be reserved weeks ahead of time), or on the summer patio that extends out over the mill pond.

The Millcroft Inn wine list is a truly global collection of fine wines, with perhaps an emphasis on French products. Whatever the meal and whatever your preference, there is something on the wine list for you: Chardonnay, sauvignon blanc, Riesling, cabernet sauvignon, Merlot, pinot noir, Gamay, champagne.

Great food is not the only reason that business groups flock to the inn. The Millcroft has a separate stone building that is fully equipped for corporate meetings. The separation of corporate and leisure guests is just one more example of the inn's courtesy. Wolfgang Stichnothe, who has over three decades of experience in hospitality in Europe and Canada, is the quintessential innkeeper, always anticipating guest needs and meeting them with prompt but invisible service. He delights in personal contact with guests and has cultivated a friendly, professional staff.

The inn's large property and its location in the Credit River valley present an opportunity to really relish our four distinct seasons. During the summer, there are walking trails, fishing and canoeing on the mill pond, tennis, volleyball and horseshoes. Mountain bikes and a tandem cycles are available for use on the property or on area roads. Choice tee times can be arranged at nearby Osprey and Caledon golf clubs. The inn can also arrange for fly-fishing adventures, horseback treks and hot air balloon rides.

The fall opens with The Arts Festival in the Hills, an ambitious ten-day celebration of the arts — visual, literary and theatrical — sponsored by the Headwaters Country Tourism Association. There is a diversity of events in a number of venues. The Millcroft Inn hosts author readings as its contribution to the festival; details are available at the front desk.

If you are fortunate enough to be at the Millcroft during autumn's brilliant foliage, then a drive through the Forks of the Credit near Belfountain is an unforgettable experience, but be warned that mid-week is recommended to avoid weekend crowds. Thanksgiving is celebrated with traditional foods, and November brings a wild game night with a six-course extravaganza of venison, pheasant, buffalo, and other full-flavoured treats. Each course is complemented by appropriate wines.

With the advent of winter, Millcroft's pine forest looks like a Christmas card scene. There are groomed cross-country ski trails on the property, and staff can provide directions to several local provincial parks and conservation areas that have additional trails (snowshoes and skis are available for guests). Caledon Hills Ski Club has nineteen of the best downhill runs in Southern Ontario, and because it is a private club with limited public ski days, it is never crowded. When our silver white winter melts into spring, the Millcroft taps its own maples and produces syrup; guests may watch the process and enjoy a maple-sweetened menu.

Regardless of the season, leisure shopping is another prime reason to visit the Alton area. Caledon Hills, Hockley Valley and the Credit River Valley are names synonymous with a day spent in the exploration of quaint towns and stores. Be sure to take in the hamlet of Glen Williams, a Credit River town with a creative art studio in its old mill, where painters, potters, weavers, glass blowers and metalsmiths display and sell top-quality items. Other towns that should be included on the country shopping tour are Belfountain, Inglewood, Mono Centre, Caledon and Hockley Village.

One of the region's art treasures is located right at the

Millcroft. The Raynes Crystal Collection, the boutique of Mark Raynes Roberts, is found on the main floor of the conference centre. Raynes is an internationally acclaimed expert in the design and engraving of crystal. There are works of sculpture, as well as delicate, detailed engravings of historic scenes, wildlife, horses and abstract images. Limited-edition prints made from details of large works are also available.

What do you get when you graft European standards onto a nineteenth-century Canadian mill? A vintage expression of sophisticated cuisine and attentive service in a setting of country-side charm.

The Millcroft Inn

55 John Street
Alton, ON
L0N 1A0
(519) 941-8111
1-800-383-3976 (Ontario only)
Fax: (519) 941-9192
Innkeeper: Wolfgang Stichnothe

52 rooms and crofts
Dining room open to the public
Directions: Drive west from Caledon on Highway 24; north on Highway 136 to Alton, and follow signs to the west end of town.
Tariffs: expensive
On site: games room, sauna, indoor whirlpool, outdoor pool and whirlpool, hiking, mountain biking, hot-air ballooning, fishing, canoeing, paddleboating, croquet, tennis, skating, cross-country skiing
Off site: antique hunting, shopping, cycling, fishing, golf, downhill skiing

SHERWOOD INN

Port Carling

The Muskoka Lakes region has graciously entertained travellers for well over a century with its winning combination of deep blue lakes, maple-covered hills and grand Victorian resorts. Although Muskoka is rapidly becoming developed and busy, there are small corners of Ontario's lakeland where you can still bask in the elegance of years gone by.

The Sherwood Inn was constructed in 1939 to replace an earlier resort that met its demise, as so many others have, by fire. John and Eva Heineck took the inn over during the late 1970s, and the inn's reputation for exceptional dining and service has never wavered since: it has received the Four Diamond Award eighteen consecutive years. Manager Philip Meyer and head chef James Saunders joined the Sherwood staff from legendary Horsted Place, in East Sussex, a number of years ago, and brought Horsted's French-inspired cuisine and country-life-with-polish along with them, making Sherwood a composite of a Muskoka resort and an English country house.

The main inn building is a postcard photo of what a Muskoka inn should be: immaculate white clapboard accented by green shutters. The inn is surrounded by stone paths lined with colourful impatiens, and covered under a canopy of century-old spruce and pine. The main guest lounge — with wood panelling, stone hearth and floral sofas — is the perfect place to while away a few hours with books, games and newspapers.

Guest rooms are found in several buildings — the inn, lakeside cottages, and the newly-constructed Maplewood. Traditionalists will want to reserve a room at the main inn. These rooms have armchairs and bedspreads in delicate hues, antique writing tables and accents, and large windows overlooking the grounds. The cottages are very private retreats, with one or two bedrooms (or a bedsitting arrangement), a wood-burning fireplace and a lovely view of Lake Joseph. The four-storey Maplewood has fourteen luxury suites, each with a wet bar, a private deck overlooking the lake, and a double whirlpool tub; some rooms also have a wood-burning fireplace. Returning guests are treated to their choice of room and dining table, and will find truffles, chocolates and champagne waiting in their room.

One of the main attractions of Sherwood is its fine food, which is described as country house cuisine with accents of the Mediterranean. The menu changes seasonally in order to capitalize on fresh ingredients, and all breads, pastries, soups and sauces are made in the kitchen. Appetizers may include Malpeque oysters with a curried bell pepper chutney, or chilled field tomato and jicama soup with pickled pink ginger and basil. Recommended main-course choices are poached darne of Atlantic salmon and wild mushroom fettuccini topped with a ragoût of lobster and mussels. The menu features many local ingredients, such as Muskoka wild mushrooms, northern lake trout, Georgian Bay whitefish and Burk's Falls pheasant.

Dessert will allow you to experience popular and oft-abused dishes prepared and presented in their true glory, such as peach tarte tatin served with homemade cranberry ice cream or the pumpkin-and-brandy crème brulée. The pan-fried tofu with macerated strawberries is an award winner (apparently the secret to success with tofu is to marinate it in maple syrup for two days).

Chef Saunders's reputation is widespread, and the inn hosts very popular cooking weekends, during which guests don aprons and grasp spatulas to learn, hands-on, the ingredients and techniques required to produce good food.

Wine connoisseurs will be pleased to know that Sherwood's cellar is well stocked, with a list of over a hundred wines from around the world. The house wines include at least half a dozen varieties of grape from several countries. Sherwood's own label is a French offering specially bottled for the inn.

While many cottage-country inns serve good dinners, breakfast and lunch often pale in comparison. Not so at Sherwood, where every meal is a celebration. Breakfast includes a selection of hot and cold cereals and fresh fruit, followed by eggs Benedict served on Saunder's signature smoked salmon, a ham and mushroom bake, pancakes and French toast. Lunch is just as lavish as dinner, with inventive homemade soups, salads and sandwiches that change daily.

Most of your time at a Muskoka resort will be spent out of doors. Sherwood has a private, sandy beach that extends at wading depth for dozens of metres. The boathouse has several rental craft, including sailboats and two high-powered inboards. The queen of the boathouse is a classic, antique wooden pleasure boat that once belonged to Lieutenant Governor John Black Aird; it is available for guided tours only. Windsurfers, canoes and non-motorized boats are available free of charge to guests. The best way to cruise is aboard the Royal Mail Ship *Segwun,* which sails from Gravenhurst on several trips daily during the summer. Lunch and dinner cruises are available, and for groups, the Sherwood staff can arrange for the *Segwun* to call in at the inn's own dock.

Golfers are thrilled that their hosts can arrange choice tee times and lessons at three championship golf courses that lie within a short drive of Port Carling. Other special days include a fly-in fishing trip or a bird-watching hike guided by experts from the Wye Marsh nature area. There are tennis courts on site, and lessons are available. Sherwood also offers facilities for badminton, croquet, horseshoes, table tennis and billiards (on a grand antique table).

Those who can't imagine leaving the gym for a few days, take heart. The brand-spanking-new Idlewood Health Club is outfitted with exercise machines, locker rooms, a sauna and a whirlpool. The whirlpool is in a separate room surrounded by large operable windows, so guests have the option of having their soak al fresco, which is a real treat during the winter.

Cyclists are only a short drive from one of Ontario's best off-road adventures. The Sequin Trail travels along the railbed of J. R. Booth's Ottawa–Parry Sound line. It is accessed at Highway 69, six kilometres south of Oastler Lake Provincial Park (parking and washrooms at the visitor information centre). The trail runs 61 kilometres, from Highway 69 to the hamlet of Fern Glen, just west of Highway 11. The western portion of the trail is a wide gravel road through typical Canadian Shield country, while the eastern portion of the trail is very flat and sandy, traversing several large wetlands. Mosquito repellent is advisable during spring and early summer, and it is wise to check on trail conditions with the Ministry of Natural Resources. The highlight of the ride is the ghost town of Seguin Falls, originally a crossroads on the notorious Nippissing colonization road. Picturesque buildings are surrounded by abundant wildflowers and flanked by the noisy river rapids, making this a choice picnic spot.

Muskoka is just as much fun during the winter, when the crowds are in abeyance and the only sound is the crackle of ice-laden boughs. Wintry quiet can be enjoyed on Sherwood's 16 kilometres of track-set, groomed, cross-country ski trails or on the floodlit natural skating rink. There is also a toboggan hill.

Muskoka is not all about athletics, of course. Port Carling is also being transformed into a first-rate shopping village, with several stores selling clothing and local crafts. Must-visits are the Muskoka Moose, for brilliantly coloured papier-mâché trays, bentwood baskets and ironwork, and the Port Carling Bakery, for luscious sweets, including a Muskoka favourite, chocolate boats. And speaking of boats, you can spend several peaceful hours on the knoll overlooking the locks at Port Carling, surveying the daily sail-past of catamarans, sailboats large and small, and luxury power cruisers. This small park is also the home of the Muskoka Lakes Museum, a treasure trove for boat aficionados, with a collection of historic photos, construction drawings and text that recounts the story of Muskoka's past as a boat-building centre.

Muskoka is tailor made for car touring. Not only is the scenery of wooded hills and small farms very pleasant, but the backroads are often the location of interesting art galleries and studios. Fall is Muskoka's most splendid season, for there's nothing quite as breathtaking as crimson, gold, and russet foliage against a background of pink granite and white birch. The entire landscape appears arranged for maximum visual impact; I recommend driving east along Highway 118.

Drive north along Regional Road 7 toward Minett to visit elegant Clevelands House resort. The twin-spired, white clapboard St. John the Baptist Church at Morinus, perched on a promontory overlooking Lake Rosseau, is, understandably, a popular subject for photographers. Autumn is also the time to savour Muskoka's ruby-red cranberries. Cranberries thrive in the region's cool temperatures, acidic peat bogs and abundant water. Bala's Cranberry Festival, held the weekend after Thanksgiving, features an art show, a cranberry breakfast at St. Alban's rectory, and fascinating tours of local growing bogs.

Muskoka has an impressive list of special events. The Parry Sound Festival of the Sound takes place for three weeks in mid-summer and attracts a large following of music lovers. The

Sherwood is one of several venues in this ever-expanding festival, so guests do not have to travel at all to take in an event. The Sherwood can arrange for outings that combine a cruise on the *Segwun* with a performance of summer-stock theatre at the Muskoka Festival, either at its traditional home at the Opera House in Gravenhurst, or in alternate quarters in Port Carling or Parry Sound.

As if all these events aren't sufficient, Sherwood Inn designs several special weekends for their guests, including photography weekends led by Bracebridge photographer Lyle McIntyre. Christmas and New Year's bring gala packages with festive decorations, foods and live entertainment.

The Sherwood Inn has a solid reputation for hosting business meetings, whether small conferences, private retreats or corporate celebrations. There are seven meeting rooms, the best being a bright, spacious room in the main inn that enjoys a wide-angle panorama of huge pines and water. Break the ice among business colleagues through Sherwood's scavenger hunts, cooking and line dancing competitions, or pig roasts and barbecues (summer or winter!). Sherwood's corporate meeting staff coordinate experiential learning programs with Delta Synergy. The inn provides the site and facilities, including a wall climbing course and a high ropes course, and the facilitators turn these activities into team-building opportunities.

Sherwood Inn is committed to providing guests with a tranquil setting, elegant dining and excellent, unobtrusive service, making this the finest hostelry in Muskoka, and well deserving of your next getaway.

Sherwood Inn

Box 400
Port Carling, ON
P0B 1J0
(705)   765-3131
1-800-461-4233
Fax: (705) 765-6668
Innkeepers: John and Eva Heineck

40 rooms

Dining room open to public

Directions: Take Highway 69 to Highway 169 South. Follow this to Sherwood Road.

Tariffs: expensive

On site: Idlewood Health Club, billiards, boating, canoeing, kayaking, windsurfing, beach, tennis, shuffleboard, ropes course and rock climbing wall, cross-country skiing

Off site: Segwun cruises, Muskoka Festival Theatre, Parry Sound Music Festival, shopping, fishing, hiking, cross-country skiing

THE VINTNER'S INN

Jordan

Individuals committed to high performance in one field of endeavor are often able to attain a similarly high standard in another calling. That is the story behind an exciting new addition to Ontario's hospitality industry. Helen Young and Leonard Pennachetti are the owners of Cave Spring Cellars, a label much favoured and discussed by wine connoisseurs. Borne by that success, they opened On the Twenty, which is consistently rated as one of the top dining rooms in the country. But energetic, competent people rarely rest on their laurels, and Young and Pennachetti decided to add an inn to the growing family of businesses. And so, The Vintner's Inn was born.

The inn is located on a side street in Jordan, the heart of Ontario's wine country, in a former winery warehouse. Cave Spring Cellars purchased the building across the street to use for winemaking during the mid-1980s and added a retail store shortly thereafter. Eventually, surrounding buildings were purchased for the restaurant, inn and shops, which means that Young now manages practically an entire village. The polish she adds to all of her projects will ensure that the inn will always be located in complementary surroundings.

The inn, protected from the busyness of street level, occupies the second and third floors of the old sugar warehouse. A long flight of stairs leads up to the main lobby and front desk, where the genteel ambience and refinement of The Vintner's Inn first starts to sink in. The colour scheme employs understated golds, greens and neutrals, the mantels, counters and tables are finished in stone, and classic columns are commonly used as accents. Luxury and comfort without ostentation is the theme.

Ten guest suites — all of which are spacious enough to entertain in — are furnished with antiques and reproductions. Some suites have two double beds, a fireplace and a whirlpool tub, and offer a view over the outdoor garden design shop at street level. Others have a lower-level living room with a gas fireplace and an upper level with a king-size bed, full bath and a whirlpool tub. Deluxe lofts are splendid, spacious suites with a lower-level living room, powder room, wet bar, refrigerator and fireplace; the upper level contains two double beds and a full bath with a whirlpool.

The inn also has business-meeting facilities. In close proximity to international airports, but a world away in terms of atmosphere, it makes an ideal, secluded retreat centre. Not only is the inn in a private setting, but its restaurant has an elegant private dining room.

You don't need to travel far for excellent cuisine. Directly across the quiet street is On the Twenty restaurant. The building, the oldest section of the original winery, dates to 1871. The restaurant is all windows on one side, taking advantage of the view over the river valley. During the summer, the scene is filled with flowers and trees, and in winter, the clear view to the skating pond far below is charming. The dining room has been finished in materials salvaged from buildings in Ontario and New York State that were undergoing demolition; marble tiles, columns and balustrades, all made from top-quality stone, have been ingeniously reused. There are several immense paintings — florals of dramatic colours and shape — that are a contrast to the pale walls. These were created by Jane Kewin of Mount Forest, whose work is also displayed in the inn.

On the Twenty earns its top reviews honestly. Chef Michael Olson makes maximum use of Niagara's bounty of fruits and vegetables. His food sources have been carefully selected for quality and organic farming methods. The menu notes these local sources: Thwaites Estates dried fruit and vinegars, Metler Road rainbow trout, Kimmer's Farm duck, and Speck Farm quails. In On the Twenty's kitchen these fine ingredients are prepared simply, with carefully chosen accompaniments. Main dishes include spit-roasted pork loin in a maple wheat-beer glaze, with red-onion relish, and veal chops under mushroom ragoût and served with green-onion potato cake. To top off these delicacies, On the Twenty picks the best of the local fruit harvest and serves up berries and cream on orange poppyseed shortcake. They also have the best-anywhere fruit cobbler, which is accompanied with Chantilly cream — life couldn't get any better.

The marriage of On the Twenty with the Cave Spring Cellars winery is a happy one. No other inn can boast the unique wine list of On the Twenty. All wines served are VQA Niagara Peninsula and represent the best vintages from several local wine makers. The list also has an extensive offering of wines exclusively made by Cave Spring Cellars for the restaurant and the winery outlet next door. The dessert wine list includes some imported ports, cognac, and several single-malt whiskeys.

Young and Pennachetti didn't stop at creating a fine restaurant and inn. They went on to create a whole village for their patrons. There is no need to go farther afield, as Young has scoured the countryside for the best in antiques, books, art, garden furnishings and holiday clothing and brought it to your doorstep. The winery buildings purchased by Cave Spring have been used for several street-level shops. In the way of home decor, three antique stores sell a broad range of antiques, from rustic Canadiana to fine European furniture. Ninavik has sculpture and wall hangings from the Arctic, the Art Vine & Books has original paintings and beautiful books on wine, and the Copper Leaf has a wonderful supply of garden-theme decorations for indoors and out. Canadian-made casual knit clothing is the theme at Tintern on Main; many patrons are eagerly awaiting the release of Tintern's own line of clothing. The Sampler Gallery is the shop for the Jordan Historical Museum, which is located high atop the Escarpment; the Sampler has changing displays and items for sale related to local history.

Wine lovers will want to head for Cave Spring Cellars's own store. It is infused, all year long, with the unmistakable tang of a sunny day during wine-making season. Black-and-white-checked marble flooring and glossy cabinetwork give the winery outlet a distinguished appeal. This isn't as much a store as it is a wine boutique, with its wide variety of Cave Spring wines and coveted ice wines, including vintages only sold here. There are wine-related items such as napkin rings, tea towels and eye-catching platters, all carrying a wine bottle or grape theme. The shop also sells videos on wine making and selection.

Winery tours leave the store daily at 2 P.M. (tours include tastings and are complimentary to inn guests). They provide an insider's look at grape growing and wine production and also emphasize the importance of the region's unique geography to wine production; this area is called the Beamsville Bench of the Niagara Peninsula, and the name has become synonymous with the best growing conditions in Ontario. Since 1986, Cave Spring Cellars has produced pure vitis vinifera wines — no blended house wines or fortified wines. Cave Spring Cellars is a founding member of the Vintner's Quality Alliance. The VQA seal indicates that this is a serious winemaker committed to high-quality growing and production. The winery produces Chardonnay, pinot noir, Riesling, Gewurztraminer, Merlot, and cabernet wines. Its 1991 Chardonnay Reserve won the gold medal at the 1995 VinItaly in Verona — proof of Cave Spring's high standards.

The Niagara Peninsula grows fruit in abundance, and although grapes may be its most famous product, harvest season is also a celebration of berries, cherries, peaches and plums. Tours of farm country may be arranged through Niagara Peninsula Agri-Tours, a local company that operates from Lake's Edge Vineyards. The tours take in vineyards, greenhouses and livestock farms, as well as some outstanding Niagara Escarpment scenery. Late September is the time to really celebrate farm country; that's when Niagara hosts a week-long Grape and Wine Festival. If independent travel is your bent, innkeeper Helen Young can suggest several routes through wine country that include winery tours and samplings and fruit markets, as well as visits to art studios and galleries. Wiley's is a family juice operation on the outskirts of St. Catherine's that produces popular pure fruit juices and blended juices. For three weeks each June they have open houses that include tours and samples.

Niagara is such a wonderful region for touring because it offers something of interest in every season. Helen Young can help guests arrange golf outings at a score of good courses nearby, and she offers cycling tours guided by a Tour de France cyclist. Both golf and cycling can be the basis of inn packages, which include accommodation, meals and a golf or cycling shirt.

While any trip to the Niagara region would be incomplete without a look at the falls, there are ways to experience the river and the gorge while avoiding the worst of the crowds. There is a paved, level path for walking, hiking, cycling and cross-country skiing that runs alongside the river from Fort Erie to Niagara-on-the-Lake. At the Niagara Glen Conservation Area, located a little north of Niagara Falls, a long staircase takes hikers to the bottom of the river gorge, where they can hike through a viny, lush forest and see immense boulders deposited by the powerful river.

Niagara offers plenty to do in wintertime. During the Festival of Lights, which is held from November to February, dozens of coloured light displays are at their sparkling best at several locations near the main falls viewing area. The best place to beat the winter blues are the Niagara Parks Commission's Conservatory, and the new butterfly conservatory. From cyclamen to forsythia, the greenhouses are filled with sweet perfume and are resplendent with colour. Add tinkling fountains and ornamental pools to the scene, and voilà, it's June in January.

Mother Nature gave Ontarians her best effort in the magnificent Niagara river gorge, the towering cliffs of the Escarpment and the fruit lands of the Beamsville Bench. Helen Young and Leonard Pennachetti celebrate this natural heritage through their excellent endeavours: Cave Spring Cellars, On the Twenty, and the luxurious Vintner's Inn.

The Vintner's Inn

3845 Main Street
Jordan, ON
L0R 1S0
(905) 562-5336
1-800-701-8074
Fax: (905) 562-3232
Innkeeper: Helen Young

10 rooms
On the Twenty restaurant
Directions: Exit the Queen Elizabeth Way at Jordan Road, and
    follow signs for Cave Spring Cellars on Main Street.
Tariffs: expensive
On site: sauna, exercise room, shopping
Off site: Shaw Festival, Niagara Falls, Jordan Historical Museum,
    shopping, winery tours, Niagara Parks conservatory, Festival
    of Lights, cycling, golf, cross-country skiing

THE KIELY HOUSE
INN & RESTAURANT

Niagara-on-the-Lake

The crack of musket fire in a pallisaded fort, a gargantuan ocean freighter an arm's length away, the sweetness of freshly made peach jam, the perfume of peonies and roses — Niagara has such an embarrassment of riches that even a brief visit will strike all the senses. The Kiely House Inn & Restaurant, in Niagara-on-the-Lake, is sheltered from Niagara's crowds and yet perfectly located to take advantage of all the region has to offer, including museums, wineries, gardens, and, of course, theatre.

Kiely House Inn & Restaurant successfully models English-inn accommodation. The Kiely House location simply can't be beat: it is on Queen Street, a short walk from the theatres and Niagara Historical Museum, and yet far enough away to guarantee a very peaceful ambience. Ray and Heather Pettit, being ex-pats themselves, looked at several communities on both sides of the Atlantic before they decided on Niagara-on-the-Lake.

The Kiely House, built in 1832 for lawyer Charles Richardson, is a large, two-storey white home, with a superb columned porch and second-storey verandah. A "new" addition was constructed in 1898. A spacious fenced property with flower gardens and verdant lawns is shaded by huge trees. The parlour, the verandah and many of the guest rooms bask in the gentle, dappled light that filters through the boughs.

The interior of Kiely House is as interesting as its formal, classical exterior. Its suspended staircase has a curved second-storey landing, and an unusual curved doorway leads to several guest rooms. That staircase and doorway, the dining room chandeliers and ornate golden mirrors above the fireplaces have all been designated as of historical importance by the local architectural conservation committee, as has the house itself. Because of this, little refinishing has been done, and the oak floors, doors and windows show their age with rustic charm.

There are fifteen guest rooms furnished with antiques and reproductions. The rooms in the oldest part of the inn are the most attractive; many have four poster beds, and some have fireplaces. The room of choice is on the main floor, occupying what would have been the original kitchen. Its focal point is a huge red-brick pioneer hearth, with the original wide pine mantel, bake oven and cooking utensils. The bed has a white frilly canopy, there is a lounging settee in front of the fireplace, and the bathroom has a Victorian claw-footed tub. Just outside the French doors is a private porch overlooking the back garden.

Many of the upper-storey rooms have wide-angle views over the golf course, which affords Kiely House valuable privacy and quiet on two sides. Several rooms have private balconies set with comfortable padded wicker furniture; others share a common verandah. It's hard to imagine a more relaxing way to spend a few hours than to sit under the trees, sip a long cool one, and listen to the cardinals sing. While everyone else is jockeying for a parking space and rushing to the theatre, Kiely House guests can linger until the last minute, and arrive cool, calm and collected.

The dining room continues the English ambience, with its green-and-yellow-flowered wallpaper and garden-green trim. A large grandfather clock keeps time, and a huge vase of yellow roses occupies a central table. Plans for the future include installing William Morris patterns and prints on the walls. The dining room is a relatively new addition to the inn, but chef Kristen Tupper and food and wine manager Claudio Marchese have quickly developed a successful working partnership. Several times a year special dinners are arranged to highlight the chef's skill, and each course is complemented by specially selected wines. All meals, including desserts, are prepared from scratch, and the inn even smokes its own salmon and chicken.

The Mediterranean taste of the goat-cheese pissaladere somehow fits perfectly with the sunny atmosphere of the house. A generous serving of warm goat's cheese sits atop marinated tomatoes, kalamata olives and basil, the whole ensemble cooked in a crisp pastry crust. The inn's signature entree is black-olive-encrusted sea bass accompanied by a warm spinach salad, oven-roasted tomatoes, scented rice cake and fennel oil. If you visit during the fall, taste the sweetness of late-season apples in the tarte tatin; the Kiely House version has an oatmeal crust and is served with gelato fresco. The chocolate dessert of choice is a rich dark-chocolate mousse with hazelnut and white-chocolate crust.

Outside of regular dining-room hours, Kiely House has a parlour menu of lighter meals that can be taken by the grey marble fireplace in the dramatic pink and black lounge. And, true to its British roots, the inn serves authentic afternoon teas daily. The traditional Victorian tea is served with finger sandwiches and a variety of small sweets. There is also a luscious Devon cream tea, and the Pettits are committed to serving only genuine Devonshire double cream with their scones and strawberry preserves. The tea chest also has a healthy supply of traditional and herbal teas that can be enjoyed with lemon or milk.

Niagara-on-the-Lake is one of the most historic and attractive towns in Ontario, and could be a holiday destination all on its own. But the Shaw Festival, which runs from May to November, is internationally renowned for its fine program of plays by George Bernard Shaw and contemporaries. The festival has three venues: the large, contemporary Festival Theatre, and the Royal George and Court House theatres, all on Queen Street.

The appreciation of things historic is an integral part of life here, and the town has numerous museums. The Niagara Historical Museum has over twenty thousand items arranged to illustrate local history from early settlement to the present, and there is a Victorian herb garden on the museum grounds. On the outskirts of town lies Fort George, a frontier military outpost with pointed wooden pallisades protecting a central parade ground and wooden buildings. This reconstructed fort (the original was founded by formidable Fort Niagara across the river), is garrisoned by costumed soldiers and citizens, who re-enact scenes of British military life.

Just south of town, on the Niagara Parkway, is Georgian, red-brick McFarland House, the only house in the area to survive the war (locals refer to the War of 1812 as "the war" as if there were no other). Used as a military hospital by both the British and American armies, it is now a museum furnished to the 1800 period, and costumed guides give tours. Another interesting home is that of heroine Laura Secord, whose daring walk through the wilderness to warn the British of a surprise American attack earned her a prominent place in Canadian history books. Her white clapboard home is furnished to period and storyboards on the grounds chronicle her life.

Niagara is not just about history. Many visitors are content to spend their time shopping on Niagara-on-the-Lake's Queen Street, where stores sell everything from clothes to fine art. Be wise and plan your trip mid-week, when crowds are less dense, or even better, arrive off-season, when the finely preserved historic main street can really be appreciated. Don't miss Greaves, makers of delicious jams, jellies and chutneys since 1927. Greaves's peach jam, made when the local crop is at the peak of perfection, is very special.

Do try to tear yourself away from the shops, however tempting they are, because the town is so wonderful for a back-street perambulation. Immaculately kept Georgian and neoclassical homes are elegantly simple, with symmetrical arrangements of doors and windows, and traditional colour schemes of black roof, white trim, and white, blue or yellow clapboard. What distinguishes Niagara-on-the-Lake from other small, historic towns with historic roots are the fabulous gardens — the town has no rival from a horticultural point of view. While garden designs vary, meticulous care and a mild climate are rewarded with luxuriant growth.

For travellers who would like to extend their touring a little farther from town, Kiely House supplies brochures on Niagara attractions, and can help guests plan a winery tour or backroads cycling adventure. Another pleasant outing is a visit by car or bike to the Welland Canal and Port Dalhousie. The best place to see the canal is at the Lock 3 Visitor Centre in St. Catharines. The canal is a busy place throughout the shipping season, and you are guaranteed to see a gigantic lake freighter (they are called "thousand-footers" for good reason) go through the locks. The St. Catharines Historical Museum is also located at Lock 3; local history is described through artifacts, text and documents, with special attention paid to the design, construction and operation of the Welland Canal.

Port Dalhousie is a lakeside town of great charm. The port was at the northernmost end of the first Welland Canals, and it was busy as a chandler's centre — a place where ships crews could buy supplies. Any town that entertained sailors had to have two features: a pub and a lock-up. Port Dalhousie had plenty of the former (seventeen according to the record books), many of which have become restaurants and fine stores. The town had one small jail, with only two cells; it stands around the corner from the Port Mansion restaurant. Later, Port Dalhousie became a popular daytrip destination for Torontonians, who would take a ferry here and ride on the carousel in the lakeside park. That carousel and its 120-year-old organ still operate during the summer, and the price for a gallop on a wooden horse remains the same: one nickel.

Port Dalhousie stills carries the exciting aura of a port. A long pier extends far out into Lake Ontario, where landlubbers can catch the scent of open water and watch the yachts dip and roll in the white caps. The marina, across the canal from the stores, is a good place to get a closer view of the yachts. It is also a good vantage from which to photograph the picturesque old portside buildings, especially at night when they wear strands of tiny white lights.

Citizens of Niagara-on-the-Lake don't just enjoy history and culture, they live and breathe them. In a town where redcoats stand at attention, and where a war fought to defend royal territory is still current news, the Kiely House Inn & Restaurant does its loyal part, providing the quiet, relaxed atmosphere of a genuine English inn.

The Kiely House Inn & Restaurant

209 Queen Street
Box 1642
Niagara-on-the-Lake, ON
L0S 1J0
(905) 468-4588
Fax: (905) 468-2194
Innkeepers: Ray and Heather Pettit

15 rooms
Dining room open to the public
Directions: Queen Street is the main thoroughfare in town, and
    the Kiely Inn is a couple of blocks west of the main
    downtown area.
Tariffs: inexpensive
On site: garden
Off site: Shaw Festival, Niagara Historical Museum, Fort George,
    McFarland House, Laura Secord house, Niagara Falls, Port
    Dalhousie, Welland Canal, winery tours, shopping, walking,
    golf

THE BRIARS

Jackson's Point

A n essential ingredient in any successful inn is a welcoming, genial atmosphere. The Briars in Jackson's Point comes by its characteristic warmth naturally: it has been home to the Sibbald family for over 120 years. Although the inn has grown to become one of the province's most popular year-round resorts, the Sibbald family and The Briars staff continue to make guests feel as if they are staying with old family friends — appreciated and gladly received.

The history of The Briars follows the story of a family, a Regency home, and an entire chapter in Ontario's development. The main inn building, now called the Manor House, was built in 1840 as an estate home on the 1200-acre land grant of retired Royal Navy captain William Bourchier. As with so many of his well-bred, well-to-do peers, Bourchier favoured the Regency style of architecture, which incorporates many characteristics that were popular in Imperial India. A two-storey, squarely built white house with symmetrically placed windows, the home's formality was relieved by a "cottagey," low, hip roof and deep eaves.

The property, named The Briars by Bourchier, came into the hands of a neighbour, Dr. Frank Sibbald, in 1878. Sibbald expanded the house, constructed the Coach House and Peacock House, and planted many of the ornamental trees — oak, spruce, cedar — that were popular in Victorian times. These trees are now magnificent, and give Briars guests the feeling of being in another world. The Briars passed through several generations of the family, each making its mark on the property. Fortunately, each generation cherished and improved their inheritance, so that modernization has not obliterated the original home.

The Briars' two areas, the Inn and the Country Club, are linked by a championship golf course and groomed walkways. The Inn is comprised of the original Bourchier home (honoured by the Ontario Heritage Foundation), which now houses guest rooms, a dining room, and recreation and business meeting facilities. The exterior face of the inn has remained largely unchanged over the decades. The interior exudes the atmosphere of early Upper Canada: the sedate library and drawing room have ancient fireplaces and authentic wallpaper; the hall stairs are lit by leaded, stained-glass windows; and all public rooms contain mementos and antiques gathered over the past five generations. The dining area is a bright space enclosed between the original home and the red-brick Coach House. Drinkwaters Lounge is a popular watering hole and gathering spot.

The Briars' best rooms are the six individually decorated guest rooms on the second and third floors of the original estate home. All rooms have gleaming pine-plank floors and spacious sitting areas, and some have fireplaces. The Green Room is suffused with gentle light from the gardens just outside, and is decorated in a floral theme — just the place to chase away the winter blahs. The names of the rooms provide a hint to their antique furnishings: for example, the Four Poster Room, the Petit Point Room, and the Canopy Bedroom.

The inn is full of quiet nooks, perfectly designed for stealing away with morning coffee, an evening nightcap, or the weekend paper (books and newspapers are supplied in abundance by The Briars). One of the most pleasurable is a charming alcove shared by the Brass Bedroom and the Four Poster Room. Another preferred hideaway is the top storey of the tower — guests are astonished to learn that the romantic tower is actually a modern addition — where sunlight streams in from every side; the view of the manicured property is expansive, and comfy couches and chairs beckon the escapee away from daily life.

The modern wings adjacent to the original Bourchier home are more contemporary, although they are decorated in the inn's deep greens, russet and florals, and have reproduction furnishings. These wings — the Bourchier and Leacock — are located near the outdoor pool and sauna; they also house the indoor pool, whirlpool, sauna and games room. The Governor Simcoe suite, luxurious and private, contains a living room and kitchenette, a whirlpool bath, and two bedrooms.

The Country Club has its own historic Club House, pro shop, swimming pool, playground and cottages. The Club House is the centre for holiday fun, which includes informal breakfasts and lunches, barbecues and children's programs. The cottages, located on wooded grounds or along the lakeshore, have fully equipped kitchenettes, televisions and fireplaces. You can practically dip your toes in Lake Simcoe from the porches of the lakeside cottages, making them very popular with families who want to be near the beach. The cottages range in size from small bed-sitting suites to family-size two-bedroom buildings, and larger. The Mayfair is perfect for family reunions, or for social and business groups. It has ten spacious rooms with views of the lake or the links, and a commodious living area with a kitchenette, fireplace, bar and plenty of seating.

While The Briars is lovely on the inside, its siting is equally impressive. Regency architecture ensures that the views toward and from the inn are long and romantic, with lots of architectural features to add interest. Overhanging boughs frame views of manicured lawns and formal gardens, and wooden chairs are placed for a perfect view of the greenery. There is plenty of space for quiet walks through the gardens or along the links, and the front desk provides bird lists (winter and summer) to help you identify some of the 140 avian species that have been seen on the grounds. The Peacock House, designated a heritage building by the Ontario Heritage Foundation, is used as a warm-up hut for skaters during the winter and as a bike lock-up during the summer.

Guest services at The Briars are exceptional. The kitchen has a reputation for country-fresh cuisine — the vegetables are grown on the premises and cooked to perfection. The menu, traditional in emphasis, typically includes excellent (and ample) prime rib, veal medallions Marsala and roast duck. The seafood chowder and hearts of palm salad don't disappoint, and neither do desserts such as homemade passion fruit ice cream and chocolate mousse gateau. Breakfast is a buffet with a large fruit salad, cereals, yogurt, and eggs prepared in a variety of ways. The Briars' Saturday-evening dinner dances have been popular for decades, and the dining room, while bright and cheerily floral during the day, is transformed into a romantic setting, with candles, fresh flowers and good music. The dining room is open to the public, but reservations are suggested, as are jackets and dresses at dinner.

The Briars is both an inn and a premier four-season resort. Guests have no need to step off the property for amusements. Golf is an important attractor, as guests have access to the private, member-owned Briars Golf Club. Here are the statistics: 18 holes, par 71, 6300 yards, and Scottish-woodlands-style design by Stanley Thompson and "Robbie" Robinson. What the stats don't tell you is that The Briars has been named one of the top fifteen small golf resorts in North America.

Because the golf course is long established, the landscaping is mature and woodsy, and wildlife sightings are common during play.

During the warm months, guests may take a leisurely cruise on The Briars' own *Lady Simcoe*, or make use of canoes, windsurfers, kayaks, sailboats, and a paddleboat. The resort has two heated outdoor pools, four tennis courts (two lighted), basketball courts (also lighted), mountain biking (including some rentals), volleyball, shuffleboard, badminton and horseshoes. The Briars even has its own private beach — a treasured commodity on Lake Simcoe. Canada's first professional summer theatre, the Red Barn Theatre, dates to the 1940s, and it is only a pleasant walk away, located in what was once the estate barn. Midweek summer barbecues are held at the Club House, and guests are encouraged to get into the spirit by dressing according to the week's theme, from roaring twenties to Caribbean.

During the winter, Lake Simcoe country sparkles blue and white, and The Briars serves up a full menu of fresh-air fun. The grounds have 10 kilometres of groomed trails, and ski-instructor Andrew Sibbald offers lessons and clinics (some equipment rentals are available). Non-skiers may skate on the ice rink (very romantic when it is lit up with twinkling lights) or on Lake Simcoe, go ice fishing, toboggan, or stay indoors and enjoy the solarium pool, whirlpool, or the fully equipped games room.

What sets The Briars apart from large resorts is the high staff-to-guest ratio, including a full-time social coordinator, sports director and instructors. When you want a tennis or golf lesson, a massage, or someone to organize your family-reunion volleyball tourney, there is someone on hand to help you. The Sibbalds know family life inside-out, and are experienced at providing the best venue for a happy holiday for everyone. During school holidays, summer and winter, kids can participate in their own special programs. Fully supervised fun is arranged for kids of different ages, and may include swimming, nature study, sleigh rides, treasure hunts, campfires and movies.

The Briars offers accommodation and meal packages for all seasons, including spring getaways, fall budget stretchers, snowman super savers, and midweek specials. Packages are often geared around special activities such as skiing and golf. Most packages include champagne or wine-and-cheese welcomers, meals, accommodations and sports events. There are also special events over Easter, Christmas, Valentine's Day and Thanksgiving.

Consider hosting your next business gathering at The Briars, which can accommodate small retreats as well as conferences. There are many comfortable meeting rooms in a range of sizes, and The Briars' corporate support staff will tailor recreation packages for each customer. Recently, the expertise of Breakthrough Associates has become part of The Briars' offerings to corporations. Classroom sessions on leadership, motivation, communication and teamwork are complemented by physical activities and challenges on The Briars grounds.

The Briars is unique in Ontario, as it offers the expansive facilities and staffing of a resort, and the gracious personal attention and deeply historic setting of a true country inn. Here's hoping that many more generations of Sibbalds commit themselves to maintaining the best in Ontario accommodation.

The Briars

Hedge Road
Jackson's Point, ON
L0E 1L0
(905) 722-3271
1-800-465-2376
Fax: (905) 722-9698
Innkeepers: John and Barbara Sibbald, with sons Hugh and
    Andrew

80 rooms and 7 cottages
Dining room open to public
Directions: Follow signs from Jackson's Point.
Tariffs: moderate
On site: sauna, games room, indoor pool, whirlpool, beach,
    windsurfing, boating, fishing, golf, cycling, badminton,
    basketball, tennis, walking, bird-watching, cross-country
    skiing, tobogganing, sleigh rides, skating
Off site: Red Barn Theatre, Sharon Temple, Sibbald Point
    Provincial Park, shopping, sailing, boating, boat cruises,
    kayaking, canoeing, ice fishing

INN AT THE FALLS

Bracebridge

Location is all important in the travel business. The Inn at the Falls has an exclusive location, perched on a cliff overlooking the roaring falls of the Muskoka River. This premiere site is made all the more appealing because the inn has recently converted neighbouring houses to accommodation, and meeting facilities. Now the entire end of Dominion Street is under the dignified umbrella of the Inn at the Falls. The result is a wonderful composite of Muskoka's beautiful outdoors and small-town charm.

Innkeepers Peter and Jan Rickard (he an Englishman, and she a native Ontarian) bring to their inn over three decades of international experience with luxury hotels (including Toronto's King Edward). They are now busy molding and fashioning the Inn at the Falls, transforming it from simply a grand old property to a classic English country inn. A British feel pervades the inn, from the authentic food and ambience of the downstairs pub, to the floral and chintz fabrics in the guest rooms, to the luxuriant perennial gardens carefully designed and nurtured by Jan.

Not all of the inn's British character comes from Rickard; the inn was constructed by English stonemasons as a spacious, red-brick house. Not long after, it became the home of William Mahaffy, the first federally appointed judge in Muskoka, and the house remained at the centre of local life for decades.

The inn's atmosphere is apparent as soon as you enter the main lobby, with its oak floors, deep wood trim and wide staircase. The main-floor parlour is familial too, with logs stacked at the ready in the fireplace, Willow-pattern china in the glassed case, and floral curtains framing a view of hydrangea and cedar. Apparently the inn is sufficiently comfortable to have convinced three earlier residents to stay permanently; just ask the innkeepers to tell the great stories about these benign spirits.

No other inn can boast the range of accommodation that Inn at the Falls can. The upper floors of the original inn have seven guest rooms, all named after local notables. Those planning a special getaway will want to book the two-storey Mahaffy suite, which has a large sitting area on a lower lever and a very private retreat at the top of the building's turret. The bathroom, with an inviting double whirlpool, and the bedroom have an eagle's view of the Muskoka Falls. Other rooms of note include the Samuel Armstrong suite, with its Queen Anne bed, living room and bar; the John Beal room, with a carved Quebec bed and a sitting area; and the golden William Mullock room, with its four poster bed. The decor throughout employs antiques, floral fabrics, ruffled curtains and bedskirts, and eyelet bed covers. Adjacent to the original inn is the Mews building, which houses ten hotel-style rooms, five with gas fireplaces, and several with skylights. Some have views over the pool and gardens, while others face the street.

Over the span of several years, the Rickards purchased all the residences at the end of Dominion Street (the street ends at the inn). This has ensured a greater measure of privacy, has added immeasurably to the range of accommodation and meeting-room space, and has given the innkeepers control over the environment surrounding their property.

The houses range in age and architecture. The cost of rooms in the houses is on par with most hotel rooms, making them a premier travel bargain. The Gate House has a private suite with a whirlpool tub and fireplace. It is hard to imagine a more perfect setting for a retreat than the English-garden Gables Cottage, which has two bedrooms, a log-burning fireplace, a wet bar and a dining area. Traveling families will want to reserve the Rose Cottage, with its full kitchen, dining room, living room with fireplace, and two bedrooms. Hammond House has three suites and three rooms; several have balconies, and one has a private garden patio. The Carriage House has a single room and three suites, each with a living room and bar, and one with a private patio.

The range of self-contained accommodation at the Inn at the Falls makes it an ideal spot for business meetings and weddings. There is a conference centre with meetings rooms, audio-visual equipment, a kitchen and washrooms.

Along with a broad range of accommodation, the inn also has a variety of eating options. Many people love the elegance of the high-ceilinged dining room. The view from the enormous picture windows encompasses the terraced lawn, which is shaded by huge maples, and far below, the river gorge and tidy town parks. Although well-appointed with Russian balloon drapery and highly polished floors, the dining room is not stiff or formal, and smart casual attire is appropriate. The diverse menu features such appetizers as Truite Poireau (trout wrapped in leek, with a white wine and dill sauce) and escargot bourguignon. Entrees include traditional standards such as steak, prime rib and seafood Wellington. House desserts in frequent demand are meringue Victoria (a perfectly baked meringue filled with ice cream, raspberry sauce and whipped cream) and turtle pie.

The dining room menu can also be enjoyed al fresco on the outdoor patio. One of summer's sweetest pleasures, dining outdoors, is made even sweeter at Inn at the Falls by Jan Rickard's green thumb. This is Canadian Shield, of course, and right where granite shoulders its way out of the ground and tree roots cling to the cliff, Jan enthusiastically plants thousands of spring bulbs, and lush cascades of phlox and daylilies among the trees.

Some people claim that the best part of Inn at the Falls is the downstairs pub, the Fox & Hounds. In fact, some travel writers describe it as one of Ontario's few credible pubs. The pub grub is superb, flavourful and plentiful, and the service is caring and friendly. On a blustery winter's day, you can warm up by the glowing fireplace with an exceptional steak and kidney pie, beer-battered fish and chips, or seafood chowder topped with camembert and puff pastry. During the summer, you can cool off with an English Double Diamond draft, and one of Ontario's best ploughman's lunches, with pickled onions, beet root, and chutney, or Scotch eggs.

Muskoka has been a vacation playland for decades. Perhaps the best day includes a cruise on the RMS *Segwun,* the last coal-fired steamship operating in North America. There are few sights as nostalgic as the white-with-green-trim *Segwun* as she sails around the headland into Gravenhurst harbour trailing a smudge of black smoke from her stack. The ship offers several cruise options, including luncheon and dinner sails, afternoon and sunset tours, and the most popular, the "Millionaire's Row" tour, which travels past the stately Victorian summer homes of the rich and famous. The brilliant orange and crimson of Muskoka's maples make a fall cruise a spectacular experience.

Gravenhurst has two other sites worth visiting. One is the large, towered Opera House Theatre, where professional theatre — mainly comedies and musicals — runs all summer. The other is Norman Bethune's parent's home, which is now a Parks Canada museum devoted to

Bethune's remarkable career as a battlefield doctor and humanitarian. The main floor of the home illustrates life at the turn of the century, while the upper storey chronicles Bethune's achievements, which include the design of medical equipment for the battlefield and his tireless efforts as a doctor and teacher in China, where he is revered to this day. It is a career worthy of tribute.

The area's best-known attraction is located right in Bracebridge: Santa's Village, where kids of all ages can fill a day with fun. The village has amusement-park rides tailored for young children, a paddlewheeler, paddle and bumper boats, and a small beach. The herd of reindeer is available for petting, and, of course, there's Santa to hug and Mrs. Claus with her cookies and other snacks. Older children head for Rudolph's Funland, where facilities include a go-cart track, minigolf, batting cages, inline skating and laser tag. Daily entertainment, video arcades and a gigantic adventure playground round out the offerings.

Bracebridge also has a unique approach to teaching history. Just below Inn at the Falls lies deep and placid Bracebridge Bay. A walking path encircles the bay, and along the path are numer- ous storyboards that describe local history, from the days of explorer David Thompson to nineteenth-century industrial development. Many of the boards include excellent historic photographs and maps that show you what the town looked like from your vantage point during the last century. Below the tiny bridge over the falls, the swirling waters of the river foam and churn with a deafening roar.

From the walkway you can climb the hill to Woodchester Villa, an octagonal home built in 1882 for mill-owner James Bird. Guided tours of the fully furnished home point out its many unusual attributes: it is made of poured concrete, has a wraparound porch and balcony, forced-air heating, indoor plumbing, electrical lighting, a speaking tube and a dumbwaiter. Considering that most habitations during the 1880s were backwoods cabins, the Villa must have been an impressive oddity.

The Inn at the Falls started off as a hostelry with a breathtaking location. Peter and Jan Rickard used their experience in hospitality and their flair for renovation and landscaping to transform it into a fine inn that is ideally situated for a Muskoka holiday.

Inn at the Falls

Box 1139
17 Dominion Street
Bracebridge, ON
P1L 1R6
(705) 645-2245
Fax: (705) 645-5093
Innkeepers: Peter and Jan Rickard

26 rooms and suites
Dining room open to public
On site: heated swimming pool
Off site: Woodchester Villa Museum, Gravenhurst Opera House,
    Bethune Museum, historic walking path, shopping in
    Bracebridge, studio tours, boating, canoeing

GRANDVIEW

Huntsville

In 1874, John Cookson purchased a large acreage in the wilds of Muskoka and began a farm, naming the property Grandview for its vantage point on a hillside by the shores of Fairy Lake. Minnie Cookson, an ambitious and hardworking woman with a nose for business, began taking in bed and breakfast guests near the turn of the century; she opened a fully operational inn in 1911. The backwoods pursuits and country cooking that attracted guests then continue to do so today, making Grandview a good choice for those exploring Muskoka.

While Grandview offers all the amenities and conveniences of a busy resort, it has, at its heart, the original Cookson farmstead. That house now serves as the dining room, and, just as Minnie Cookson's home cooking was one of the virtues of her Grandview, the modern-day inn also offers a hearty meal to its guests. The dining room overlooks the restful waters of Fairy Lake. During the winter, the antics of chickadees and grosbeaks at the feeder provide pure entertainment. Each dining room has a fireplace, antique tables, pressed-back chairs, striped wallpaper and floral balloon curtains.

Grandview's clam and peppercorn chowder is a recommended starter, and it may be followed by an ample mixed grill of lamb, game sausage, provimi liver and beef tenderloin, and decadent desserts. The inn serves a full breakfast, and the baked goods produced in the kitchen take centre stage. Raisin French toast and banana pancakes are specialties, but there are also eggs Benedict, omelettes and continental breakfast items. On summer weekends, casual fare is available at the Dockside Restaurant, and the Owl's Nest Lounge serves up evening entertainment along with cocktails.

Grandview is one of the province's best bets for travelling families. Not only is there a host of kid-tested activities on site, but whoever designed the guest accommodations understands family life. Each of the twenty signature suites has a living room with a fireplace and pullout sofa, a fully equipped kitchenette, a separate bedroom and a bathroom with a whirlpool tub. There are also seventy-five luxury suites located in seven buildings, which are spacious and well decorated, and feature a full kitchen and dining area, a living room with a fireplace and pullout sofa, a bathroom with a whirlpool tub, and a separate bedroom. The luxury suites are interconnected with the inn's sixty resort rooms (standard hotel-style rooms), so that they can be expanded to become two- or three-bedroom apartments.

Some guests at Grandview never leave the property, for even a week's vacation wouldn't exhaust all the possibilities here. Many guests head straight for the active waterfront area, where swimmers can choose between the heated swimming pool and the cool water of Fairy Lake. At the dock, there are paddleboats, windsurfers, sailboats and canoes. The cruise boat *Spirit of Muskoka* provides daily tours. Other on-site recreation facilities include a nine-hole golf course, tennis courts and a recreation centre that includes an indoor pool, sauna, indoor tennis court, games room and rental shop (with cross-country skis and mountain bikes). The inn's own trails are suitable for hiking and cycling. The paved Fairy Lake trail leads from Grandview right into the heart of Huntsville.

The Muskoka Festival Theatre presents evening performances at Grandview on Wednesdays throughout the summer. The afternoon matinee is for children, and the evening show is a musical revue. These performances take place in the Conference Centre, a business facility complete with conference and meeting rooms of all sizes.

Although historically a lumbering region, Muskoka's real bounty is in its scenic beauty and four dramatic seasons, which together provide endless opportunities for enjoying the outdoors. Grandview earns full marks for having a full-time resident naturalist on staff, Robin Tapley, whose sole purpose is to tailor wilderness experiences to the age, fitness level and inclination of each guest. Robin Tapley's nature centre, located in the inn, is fully equipped with field guides, binoculars, mosquito-proof clothing, rain gear and a host of other conveniences.

Algonquin Park is the focus of Tapley's off-site programs, and because he has lived all his life in nearby Dorset, he is fully familiar with the best canoe routes and hiking trails. He guides canoe trips for paddlers of all skill levels, and the inn has its own trolley that carries guests and up to eight canoes to the park. For overnighter trips, the inn can arrange for necessary camping gear. Tapley's familiarity with the park means that he can take his charges to lesser-known locations for wildlife viewing; on one of his "moose caboose" treks he encountered 118 moose in one day.

Fall freeze-up doesn't stop the naturalist program at Grandview, and Tapley waxes lyrical about taking guests on snowshoe and cross-country ski treks to hear barred owls, and guiding a dogsled expeditions through a silent, white environment seldom seen by tourists. Birdwatching events take place daily — and nightly — on the Grandview property, and there are scheduled bird-of-prey demonstrations. Nature-based art programs include woodcarving, moccasin making, painting workshops and wildlife photography safaris. Grandview's nature program can also be tailored to meet the needs of corporate and social groups.

Tapley's on-site programming for kids is superb. There are nature camps daily during holiday periods. On guided hikes, children from six to twelve years of age are taught to use dip nets (to capture, identify and release wetland critters), fill bird feeders, build bird boxes and identify animal tracks in the snow. The emphasis in the camps is on environmental stewardship and habitat protection. Tapley's efforts have resulted in a program to improve waterfowl habitat on Fairy Lake and to limit the environmental impact of Grandview's golf course on the lake.

Wintertime at Grandview is especially pretty, as the golf course and roadway trees are decorated with over twenty thousand twinkling white lights. Groomed and track-set ski trails traverse the golf course. The Grandview trolley that carries canoeists to Algonquin in the summer takes skiers to nearby Hidden Valley Highlands ski club during the winter. Huntsville's cold temperatures and abundant snowfall are dependable, so Hidden Valley can guarantee a long season, short lift lines and reasonable prices.

Arrowhead Provincial Park, located 8 kilometres north of Grandview, is sometimes forgotten in the shadow of its more glamorous neighbour, Algonquin, but it has its own charms. Without a doubt, it has Southern Ontario's best toboggan run. Each winter, park staff create a kilometre-long pathway of packed snow on one side of a very steep and twisty park roadway. The slide has banked sides for safety, and the other half of the road is used for sledders returning uphill (and that's plenty of exercise for the day). While some visitors bring their own equipment, the park supplies immense inner tubes and long strips of plastic sheeting free of charge. The former provide comfortable and controlled fun and the latter a fast and furious ride. The park has several hiking trails, which are good bets for wildlife viewing. During the winter, these trails are track-set and groomed for skiing. They range in length from 1 to 9 kilometres, and in difficulty from beginner to advanced. There is also a trail for walkers and snowshoers that travels to Stubb's Falls, on the Little East River.

Muskoka is not just for the fan of backwoods exploration. The area near Grandview has several other attractions worth investigating. The Muskoka Pioneer Village, in Huntsville, has fourteen buildings typical of a nineteenth-century frontier village. Costumed interpreters portray family life in the Darling log cabin and in Reverend Hill's more comfortable home. Hay General Store, Orange Hall, Wesley Church and Spence Inn make up "downtown" Muskoka. The village celebrates several special events, such as a Victorian Christmas, a maple syrup celebration (chefs from the Deerhurst Inn cook up maple-syrup cuisine over fragrant fires), a strawberry social, and a summer market day.

Life in Muskoka is not all that different from that portrayed at the village. Log cabins have been converted to upscale cottages, but a scenic backroad tour reveals several villages largely unchanged by the passing decades. Portage and Baysville are two such villages. In Baysville, visit the park by the falls, and another local landmark, Langmaid's Store. Just east of Baysville is the hamlet of Norway Point, with its photogenic white clapboard church. Just across the deep blue waters of Lake of Bays lies the island site of Bigwin Inn. This luxury hotel and resort entertained an elite international clientele until the 1940s. It now lies completely intact but unused, a ghostly remnant from the glory days of grand summer holidays.

Dorset is a daytrip destination for all seasons. During the summer, shoppers visit Robinson's General Store, advertised for miles around as Canada's best country store. Typical of general stores throughout the north, it sells souvenirs, hip waders, groceries, screwdrivers and fishing bait. During the fall, locals and tourists puff their way up the Dorset fire tower for an inspiring panorama of rolling hills — a tapestry of green pine, crimson maple and russet oak. And every winter, snowmobilers make weekend treks along the frozen lakes, ending their day with a meal at the Tom Salmon Inn.

Perhaps Muskoka's most unusual attraction is the Dwyer Memorial (it is located quite close to Grandview, but a local map and directions would be helpful). The ride in to the site is exciting, as the gravel road climbs and descends steep ravines with no guardrails. Each valley has its own rushing creek, and, in the forest, white birch stand in contrast to deep green pine and granite boulders. The Dwyer Memorial is a tall stone obelisk established as a memorial to Betsy Dwyer, beloved wife of Chicago businessman Clifton Dwyer. This is a most peculiar site, with well-manicured lawns, flower gardens and ornamental ponds — a sharper contrast to the surrounding wilderness couldn't be imagined. After spending many happy vacations in the vicinity, the couple decided that this would be their final resting place. Their ashes are contained in the two copper urns at the top of the tower, and the surrounding park is maintained by their estate.

John and Minnie Cookson may have never envisioned the present-day Grandview, with its golf course, apartment suites and canoe trolley, but they would certainly have been pleased with how people from far and wide seek out this unique combination of stellar nature programs and creature comforts.

Grandview

R.R. 4
Huntsville, ON
P0A 1K0
(705) 789-4417
Fax: (705) 789-6882
Innkeeper: Bruce Evans

168 rooms and suites
Dining room open to the public
Directions: The Grandview is off Highway 60, east of Huntsville.
Tariffs: moderate
On site: indoor pool, exercise room, games room, sauna,
    outdoor pool, canoeing, boating, boat cruises, fishing, golf,

nature day camp for kids, tennis, paddleboats, sailing, waterskiing, playground, cycling, skating, cross-country skiing, tobogganing

Off site: canoeing, nature programs, hiking, horseback riding, dogsledding, tobogganing, cross-country skiing

EGANRIDGE
INN & COUNTRY CLUB

Fenelon Falls

Picture this. Shimmering lakes rich in pickerel and bass, art studios tucked away in pine woods, luxury yachts moored by historic locks. Now, put yourself in this picture through a tour of the Kawartha Lakes region that includes delightful villages and natural beauty. For many travellers, a visit to the Kawarthas is enhanced by the gracious hospitality at the Eganridge Inn & Country Club. Eganridge is located on the shores of Sturgeon Lake, between Bobcaygeon and Fenelon Falls.

Dunsford House, the core of the Eganridge estate, is a unique combination of English design and rugged Canadian materials. Dunsford is constructed of honey-coloured, 22-inch pine timbers taken from this very site, and has a gabled cedar-shake roof. The approach to Dunsford House is as charming as its front face, for the immaculate lawn is enclosed by a hedgerow of graceful maples and a fieldstone fence.

The house, considered one of the best examples of its architecture in North America, was built in 1838 for Reverend James Dunsford. The Dunsford family was active in the local (and lucrative) lumber trade, but gradually moved away from the area. The property was eventually turned into accommodations and a golf course, but it didn't realize its potential until John and Patty Egan, with decades of experience in the hospitality industry, purchased it and began extensive renovations. John Egan is a gracious, gentle innkeeper, a master of polished yet informal customer service.

Dunsford House has six beautifully appointed luxury suites and several spacious meeting rooms with audio-visual equipment for business meetings and other events. The suites are spacious bedsitting rooms, with reproduction furnishings, an entertainment centre hidden in an armoire, and king- or queen-size beds. The bathrooms are equally spacious and have whirlpool tubs. Dunsford House has a number of cozy nooks for reading, as well as a second-storey balcony with a lake view — a perfect place for morning coffee. Guests are welcome to prepare a late-night snack or early-morning coffee from the kitchen on the main floor of the building.

Eganridge also has five cottages (some with one bedroom and one bath, and some with two bedrooms and two baths), which are popular with business and wedding parties as well as with groups of couples. The cottages have decks overlooking the lake and have wood-burning fireplaces.

Eganridge has the best dining room in the region — hence its popularity. Swiss-trained chef Alfred Keller has been at Eganridge for years, and he creates a menu with both traditional dishes and California-influenced lighter items. The club specialty is escargots en croute, which acts as an introduction to grilled sea bass with sun-dried tomato and chive, rack of lamb with dijon and rosemary glaze, or cajun style shrimp with fusilli. Eganridge desserts are high-octane treats such as chocolate-mousse pâté served with light espresso sauce and fresh fruit. The wine list has both domestic and foreign wines, and the markup per bottle is very modest.

Keller's midday meals are as diverse and well-prepared as his dinners. For lunch you can choose from three-egg omelettes, soups and sandwiches. Ingredients change seasonally; for example, an asparagus and ham omelette is available during the spring, and red-pepper soup is served late in the summer. The dining room is in the original estate barn, which has its wide balcony protected by near-invisible mosquito netting, for summer dining (this clever idea is one that should be imitated elsewhere). In spring and fall, guests move indoors to sit by the fireplace.

Most guests come to Eganridge for the golf. The course, described by some designers as having the prettiest site in Ontario, is a 3,000-yard, nine-hole facility constructed in the English style. There are plenty of sand and water hazards, and almost every tee and green offers a good view of the lake. The pro shop has a full supply of rental equipment, including carts, as well as a licensed snack bar.

While golf is the main attraction, guests can participate in several other activities at Eganridge, including a few matches on the new tennis court. The roadways on and off site are good for cycling, as they are generally uncrowded and level. A tour through the cottage community of Sturgeon Point offers particularly pleasant, shaded cycling. The inn has several waterfront facilities for its guests. There is a small, secluded beach and a marina. The innkeepers are happy to arrange fishing and sailing charters for their guests, with advance notice. They can also book tickets at the Academy Theatre in Lindsay.

There are many delightful Kawarthan villages to visit on daytrips from Eganridge. Fenelon Falls, which calls itself the "Jewel of the Kawarthas," has all the shopping and historic sites that daytrippers love. Mary, Colborne and Francis Streets are especially appealing, with dozens of brightly painted and neatly kept historic houses that have been converted to gift, clothing and antique stores.

Fenelon Falls seems designed for a leisurely stroll. The falls and the lock are always a central attraction, and you can watch the boat traffic, or select a boat cruise from the several offered. Be sure to walk along Oak Street, where Victorian mansions and huge trees look much as they did a century ago. Maryboro Lodge, located at the end of Oak Street, was built in 1837 for town-founder James Wallis. It is now a museum with over 3,500 items collected from local families.

Bobcaygeon is another town high on the list of daytrip possibilities. Like Fenelon Falls, Bobcaygeon has a lock on the Trent-Severn recreational waterway, so there are always boats passing through. Bobcaygeon and the surrounding area is a hotbed for the visual arts. Located in the heart of town are three galleries: Off the Wall (light-hearted art as well as wildlife prints), Frame of Mind and Bobcaygeon Fine Art. But the best place to find an undiscovered talent is in the gallery at the town library; the prices are modest enough to allow for more than one purchase. Studio hopping in the countryside will allow you to speak to artists in their own habitat, and perhaps see them at work. Two interesting places to visit are the Illini Gallery (on the same street as the Bobcaygeon Library), and the Chuck Burns studio (just south of town on County Road 17). Karl Illini specializes vintage automobiles and historic buildings on immense canvases, while Burns produces evocative scenes of rural life.

The town of Buckhorn, which has a number of extraordinary galleries, is known for the legendary Buckhorn Wildlife Art Festival held each August. Although the festival, which attracts thousands of serious collectors from around the globe, garners the most press, Buckhorn's galleries may be visited any time of the year. There are several galleries hidden in the verdant woods and down back lanes throughout the area; just keep your speed down so that you can respond to the roadside signs. Be sure to visit Gallery on the Lake, east of Buckhorn. The building is an octagonal structure several storeys high, hidden among the pines on the shore of Lower Buckhorn Lake. The artwork here includes Raku pottery, soapstone and jade sculpture, needlework and hundreds of acrylic and watercolour paintings.

A tour of the Kawarthas would be incomplete without a visit to the Curve Lake Reserve, located south of Buckhorn, on Highway 507. Although there are many art galleries and shops in this Ojibwa community, the main attraction is the Whetung Gallery, a huge wooden building with totem poles on either side of the entrance. Traditional Aboriginal works such as birchbark boxes decorated with porcupine quills and beaded moccasins are on display, as well as an astounding variety of paintings and sculpture with contemporary themes. Right next door to the gallery is a café that serves light meals of corn soup, Indian bread and buffalo burgers.

The Kawarthas is not all quaint villages and art galleries; it is also a region rich in lakes and forests. One of the best places to take a hike in a natural setting is at Emily Provincial Park. The Park is located on the Pigeon River, and is reached off County Road 10. (Put together a satisfying picnic lunch at one of Ontario's best small-town bakeries — Graham's, in Omemee. Sausage rolls, meat pies and salads are just an appetizer for sweet treats such as raspberry neopolitans, rumballs, and fern tarts.)

Regardless of your fitness level, you will enjoy the level, 1-kilometre Boardwalk Trail, which will bring you to within close proximity of an osprey nest perched on a nesting platform constructed by park staff. The trail takes walkers through the heart of a cattail marsh, where marsh wrens and common yellowthroats sing incessantly, turtles bask on partially submerged logs, and the weird call of the American bittern may be heard during the evening. Emily Provincial Park offers many other ways to delight in the local landscape. Canoeing on Pigeon River is popular, and there are equipment rentals from several outfitters located near the park entrance. Anglers are happy to ply the waters for some of the area's famous bass and muskie, and swimmers and sunbathers stake their claims on the beach.

The Kawartha Lakes region has been entertaining travellers for about a century and a half, and still offers a diversity of delights, from boating and backroads cycling to art galleries and summer-stock theatre. Likewise, the wide experience of the Egans and their staff allow Eganridge Inn & Country Club to offer guests a special historic property, a challenging golf course, fine dining, and warm, personable service.

Eganridge Inn & Country Club

R.R. 3
Fenelon Falls, ON
K0M 1N0
Tel & Fax: (705) 738-5111
Innkeepers: John & Patty Egan
Open April-December

11 rooms and cottages
Dining room open to the public
Directions: From Fenelon Falls, drive east along County Road 8.
  Follow signs to Eganridge.
Tariffs: moderate
On site: golf, fishing, boating, canoeing, walking, tennis, beach
Off site: Academy Theatre, Victoria County Historical Museum,
  art studios and galleries, shopping, boating and boat cruises,
  fishing, cycling, hiking

Sir Sam's Inn

Haliburton

From the moment you set foot on the wide front porch and step across the threshold onto the flagstone lobby floor, Sir Sam's Inn feels like home. Such an atmosphere isn't just coincidence; it is the result of meticulous staff training and careful choices in site and decor. In the living room, subtle lighting and antique furnishings around a glowing hearth provide an intimate setting, and the barman from the pub across the hall occasionally checks to see that guests have all they need.

Sir Sam's takes its name from Sir Samuel Hughes, Canadian Minister of the Militia during the First World War. Sir Sam selected this large acreage on Eagle Lake for his summer home, and construction was complete in 1919. The exterior appears much as it did then, a large, informal home with a stone foundation and a half-timbered second storey. The exposed beams and carefully fitted stone of the inn's principal public rooms are evidence of skilled craftsmanship. The home was first a fishing lodge and then an inn, but did not enter its renaissance as a sophisticated retreat until it was purchased and extensively renovated by innkeeper James Orr in 1979. Since that fortunate purchase, a new wing and lakeside chalets were added to the original residence.

The pub is decorated with photographs and memorabilia of Sir Sam. Hughes's career was notorious for many things, among them the controversy surrounding the Ross rifle, used by Canadian troops during the war. The rifle was a good design on paper, but its use resulted in many battlefield casualties, as it would often jam during use. As manufacturer of the rifle, Hughes became embroiled in a major political debacle. Sir Sam's own rifle rack and regimental coat of arms are incorporated into the bar at the pub. The bar is always stocked with snacks, and during winter weekdays, when the dining room is closed for lunch, the pub has a supply of soup and sandwiches to enjoy.

Sir Sam's twenty-five rooms are located in several buildings. The original residence has four very special rooms on the upper storey, called the Lakewinds Suites, which are furnished in authentic Canadiana. The corner suite, typical of these rooms, elicits an appreciative "ahhh" from arriving guests. A pine chest by the corner fireplace displays a selection of books and magazines. Seating is plentiful, and arranged for enjoying the sunshine, which can stream in from two directions. The built-in cupboard above the fireplace discreetly hides an entertainment centre. A writing table, bar fridge, and huge bed with plenty of pillows completes the main room. In the bathroom there's a huge whirlpool and an abundance of top-line toiletries. Another of the original rooms, Sir Sam's Suite, boasts its own screened-in porch that overlooks the lake.

The addition to the main building contains several hotel-style rooms. While the spacious lakeside chalet units have a modern look, they also have cathedral ceilings, expansive windows, loft bedrooms, whirlpool tubs and fireplaces. Some even have full kitchens, which make them great for travelling families.

The inn staff pay well-mannered attention to each and every guest. Those who desire a guided bike ride or a hike through the best local trails have resident manager Michael Berrisford at their service. Even the inn dog, Cody, a golden retriever, has been trained to visit each lounge guest with quiet professionalism; his leash hangs by the door for guests who want a canine companion for their strolls. The attractive inn newsletter has a guest-appreciation column, along with feature articles on upcoming events, staff news, local attractions, and a recipe from head chef Chris Baux.

Baux's kitchen produces a consistently excellent dining experience, and the food at Sir Sam's is a good part of the reason guests return season after season. The dining room, which offers a sweeping view of the lakefront, features an interesting double-sided fireplace. A dinner at Sir Sam's might begin with a flavourful lentil soup or baby greens, with smoked duck and cider vinaigrette. For a main course, don't miss Sir Sam's succulent and pink rack of lamb, served on a platter-sized plate in order to accommodate an impressive medley of vegetables and garnishes. White-chocolate lasagna, raspberry crème brulée and tartufo are some of the dessert choices. During dinner, the dining room is candlelit and romantic, but at breakfast, guests luxuriate in radiant sunlight. There is a breakfast buffet of fruit, cereals, and freshly-baked sweet breads, as well as a good choice of omelettes and other items from the menu.

This is one inn where the quality of the wine cellar can match the cuisine. Managers Michael Berrisford and Tim Baxter sparkle with delight when guests request a tour of the newly-constructed stone cellar, which is accessed via a curving wrought-iron staircase. They personally order each wine and are happy to provide guests with advice on vintages and a taste test.

Even though there are no formal recreation programs at Sir Sam's, there are enough things to do on the inn property that you could have a full holiday right here. For summertime fun there are tennis courts, a fitness trail, an outdoor pool and whirlpool, and a waterfront area with waterskiing, sailing, kayaking and canoeing. The management are particularly proud of the *Lady Hughes*, a teak launch custom made in Goderich. Guests are taken back to the elegance of the nineteenth century as they repose under the striped canopy and take in a midday, cocktail-hour or sunset cruise. During inclement weather, move indoors to enjoy the atrium exercise centre and a sauna, or table tennis and billiards.

Recreation opportunities abound in Haliburton, and Sir Sam's is close to some of Ontario's premier mountain bike and hiking trails. The Haliburton Forest & Wild Life Reserve comprises 23,000 hectares of Haliburton forest and fifty lakes. Dozens of kilometres of mountain bike trails run up and down spectacular hills. The base camp area, just inside the reserve entrance, has a cafeteria, a bike wash, an on-duty mechanic, canoe and bike rentals, and loads of trail maps.

Along with mountain-bike trails, the reserve offers scenic overlooks, secluded canoeing, and the area's best lake trout and bass fishing. Reserve staff run a program of nature-interpretation walks and talks. The reserve may be best known for its wolf centre, which includes exhibits on wolves, a theatre, and an observation room where visitors may watch the resident wolf pack in its forested enclosure.

Another location with maintained mountain bike trails is the Moosewood Trail Centre. Located a short drive from Sir Sam's, this new facility is designed especially for superb off-road cycling. There are bike rentals (see just how good a high-performance bike can make you look) and an on-site mechanic, and trails maps are available.

Winter brings breathtaking beauty to Haliburton. There is skating right in front of the inn, on Eagle Lake, and guests can also take part in snowshoeing, dogsledding and long-distance snowmobiling experiences. The latter, including a guide, equipment, and necessary clothing, takes you on a 100-kilometre, six-hour hour run through back country you'd never see on your own.) Front-desk staff can also arrange for guests to travel the backwoods using Finn sleds, which have seven-and-a-half-foot runners and are propelled by the feet like scooters. The sleds are crafted by a local toymaker and are a novel and efficient way to get around in the snow.

One of the best ways to appreciate pristine winter woodlands is to cross-country ski. The Haliburton Nordic Ski Trail Association maintains 160 kilometres of cross-country terrain, including a loop that will challenge even those who perform at an Olympic level. The Haliburton Forest & Wild Life Reserve's hiking and bike trails become ski trails during the winter, and the reserve provides warm-up shacks with fire-making supplies. The perfect place to relax those tired muscles after a ski is in the inn's outdoor whirlpool, which remains open and steamy all winter long.

Much of the incentive for a winter visit to Sir Sam's is Sir Sam's Ski Area, only a five-minute drive away. Although the two entreprises were once under common ownership, they are now separate. The ski area is run by the Bishop family, who have dedicated themselves to maintaining a ski facility with the uncrowded conditions of a private club, but with a fun, family orientation. Decades ago, a provincial government study identified the Haliburton hills as having prime ski resort possibilities. If length of season is any indication, the study was bang on. From early December until April, Sir Sam's Ski Area provides twelve runs (beginner to advanced) and six lifts, full snow-making and grooming, a mogul course, and two death-defying cliffs for Warren Miller wanna-bes. Although a 107-metre elevation isn't exactly a Rocky Mountain high, the club provides uncrowded skiing, a couple of long, woodsy trails (760 metres is the longest), well-laid-out hills that separate skiers of differing abilities, and good clubhouse facilities. The ski school employs twenty-four certified instructors, including several who have attained their Level 4 status. There is no night skiing at Sir Sam's, and the hill is closed Monday and Tuesday, except during holiday periods.

No matter what the season, Sir Sam's Inn has a special package designed just for you. Autumn's red wine and wild game weekends are very popular; between skeet-shooting contests and roaring fires, you'll enjoy Merlots, pinot noirs and cabernets, which complement the culinary magic Chris Baux works with ostrich, venison and wild boar. The inn has a spring blues weekend that features live entertainment and more fine food. Midweek specials are attractively priced all year, but especially during the winter, when ski-lift tickets are included with accommodation. Guests may enjoy spectacular fireworks displays over Eagle Lake on Victoria Day, Canada Day and New Year's Eve. Sir Sam's is also perfect for meetings, small conferences and retreats.

James Orr set a goal of creating an inn that feels just like home. But once you've enjoyed a superb meal and relaxed in a cozy nook by the hearth, after a day of soft adventure in the great outdoors you'll wish this were your home. Imagine a whole weekend.

Sir Sam's Inn

Eagle Lake Post Office
K0M 1M0
(705)   754-2188
1-800-361-2188
Fax: (705) 754-4262
Innkeeper: James Orr

25 rooms and chalets
Dining room open to public
Directions: From village of Haliburton, take Highway 118 to
    Eagle Lake and follow signs.
Tariffs: moderate
On site: billiards, table tennis, exercise room, sauna, outdoor
    pool, outdoor hot tub (year round), fitness trail, launch
    cruises, canoeing, sailing, fishing, waterskiing
Off site: mountain biking, hiking, fishing, dogsledding, downhill
    and cross-country skiing

DOMAIN OF KILLIEN

Haliburton

When you arrive at the Domain of Killien, it is like the curtains have gone up on a wonderful piece of theatre. The experience requires you to suspend your belief in order to fully appreciate what you are about to see: a Parisien bistro hidden within an Ontario wilderness resort.

Part of the Domain's unusual character is derived from its remarkable history. This property, located between the village of Haliburton and Algonquin Park, was a private fishing and hunting lodge developed by local physician Lewis Carroll. Certainly the Domain appears to be a well-groomed version of the classic Northern Ontario lodge. As you round the last bend in the gravel roadway, your first glimpse of the Domain is of deep-brown log cabins with freshly painted white chinking and, depending on the season, neat flower beds or deep drifts of dazzling white.

In 1982, the Count and Countess de Moustier purchased the camp. Count Moustier is a descendant of one of France's oldest aristocratic families; the Countess is a former ballerina with the Jazz Ballet of Harlem. The family had previously purchased the adjacent 5,000-acre parcel of land to incorporate with its forest-management holdings. The first move of the new owners was to reduce the lodge's guest capacity by fifty percent, so that it now accommodates a maximum of fourteen couples. This unusual approach to upgrading has proven most successful, for one of the delights of the Domain of Killien is its very exclusiveness. The sons of the Countess, Dante and Jean-Edouard Larcade, left France to join the business, Dante as head chef, and Jean-Edouard as innkeeper. The inn was renamed the Domain of Killien after the family's seigniorial home in Brittany, "Quillien."

While this history is sufficiently curious, there is yet more. The inn is one of only a half-dozen Canadian members of the prestigious Relais du Silence group of fine country houses. Each member is committed to warm and personal attention, comfortable accommodations with character, and a calm atmosphere without the intrusion of radios, televisions or other peace-breakers. While many Ontario resorts have gone the route of pushing back the wilderness to make way for recreation facilities and hectic programming, the innkeepers again chose the path less travelled, and guarantee guests blissful serenity.

The main inn building is full of homey charm, and the living room is a scene straight out of pioneer days. A sweetly-scented fire crackles in the enormous stone hearth, and guests can read, nap, and play table games and cards. The walls are decorated with reproductions of nineteenth-century woodcuts depicting West Indies sugar and indigo plantations, a reminder of the Moustier's family history as landowners in Guadaloupe.

Although the Domain of Killien is a family enterprise, it is Jean-Edouard's cheery disposition and polished manners that set the Domain apart from other woodsy hostelries. He vigilantly maintains the living room fire at just the correct burn, serves guests from the tea and coffee table (which is always freshly stocked), and quietly sees that every visitor has all he or she needs to "master the fine art of doing nothing, beautifully."

There are five guest rooms in the inn and several lakeside cottages, the cottages offering more privacy and the inn greater atmosphere. Inn rooms are rustic yet very comfortable, with arm chairs, large beds with lofty duvets, and a window with floral curtains. The view of sunlight glinting off the water or ice of Drag Lake is truly refreshing, as is the morning chorus of birds, which nest in every tree and under each eave of the inn. Each room includes a kettle for making tea and coffee, and a writing desk. The bathrooms have a separate cedar-panelled dressing area complete with terry robes, and a whirlpool tub. The tiling is crisp French blue and white, and the terra cotta flooring is polished to a high gloss.

The cottages are large bed-sitting rooms, with carpeting, ample seating around the fireplace, and a verandah overlooking the lake. There's an interesting story behind the naming of the cottages: Moustier was determined that if he was going to live his life in the backwoods of Ontario, that he would surround himself with at least the names of French women. Guests are awed by the complete tranquillity of both the inn rooms and the cottages, and appreciate the difference a deep, rejuvenating sleep can make.

The dining room has a more sophisticated ambience than the rest of the inn; blue jeans would not do justice to Dante's kitchen. Dante left his own bistro in Paris to manage the kitchen at the

Domain and he has been so successful that some folks have purchased cottages on Drag Lake in order to visit the dining room more frequently. Although the preparation and presentation are French, many ingredients for the kitchen are regional, with wild mushrooms and leeks, and organically grown herbs and vegetables from the kitchen's own garden.

Each dinner menu includes a choice of two appetizers, two entrees and two desserts. Appetizers may include leek-and-potato soup, or an amazing tomato tart. Favoured entrees include a perfectly-cooked pike, and grilled breast of Muscovy duck in a blackberry sauce. The portions are reasonably sized, so diners can really relish the desserts, which include a rich and warm chocolate mousse and stewed strawberries served with strawberry sorbet.

Breakfast presents more of the inn's delightful incongruencies. You sit by a frosted window watching the feeder-side antics of chickadees. The interior scene is straight from a sidewalk café. The hot chocolate is laced with nutmeg; the coffee is strongly brewed, European style; the oven-warm croissants are the genuine article; and the wall posters are distinctly Parisien (borrowed, in fact, from Dante's own bistro).

Although the dining room does not serve lunch, during the summer a light menu is available on the patio. But you may want to take advantage of the Domain's backpack lunches. Depart for the hiking and cross-country ski trails with a full pack, and return at the end of the day with an empty one.

It is no surprise that the wine cellar at the Domain of Killien emphasizes French products. Jean-Edouard selects each and every bottle of wine himself to ensure that each wine-growing region is represented and that within each region there are several choices in vintage and price.

The Domain has several interesting events for guests. Degustation weekends, which showcase both the cellar and the kitchen, are so popular with regular guests that they are usually fully booked well in advance. The agenda for such an event is a Tour de France for the palate: consommé à l'essence de pigeon truffe, foie gras en croûte, pigeon rôti aux Airelles, cuissot de chevreuil à la framboise, and a finale of fondant aux chocolats. Each course is married with specially selected premium wines. The aforementioned dinner, for example, would include red and white wines from Bourgogne and Bordeaux. Dessert is served with champagne, and the evening closes with cognac. These weekends, often led by wine importer John Sainsbury, are done in true Domain style, which puts a premium on enjoyment.

Christmas is celebrated with a fully trimmed inn and tree, and Santa Claus arrives by dogsled with gifts for the guests. New Year's at the Domain is black tie, but not too stuffy, and like the degustation weekends, features superb food and wine. Springtime brings Dante's cooking school to Haliburton, and regular chefs Christophe Letard and Christophe Delamarre instruct guests on the preparation of gourmet dinners. Autumn's special weekend events include a game and wine dinner.

But the Domain offers more than just food retreats. The unique property — thousands of hectares of unspoiled forest and lakes — is magnificent beyond words. Photography weekends assist participants to capture unique images of the beauty of this wild beauty. There are also regularly programmed nature hikes, which are led by naturalists including R.D. Lawrence.

The glorious landscape and its solitude are at the heart of the Domain of Killien. The Domain's commitment to serenity means that guests have access to sailboards, rowboats, canoes and a sailboat are available, no motorboats are permitted. Drag Lake has several sandy beaches and a natural marsh, as well as many spots for a tranquil read. Some of the Domain's lakes are stocked with bass and brook trout, and there are rowboats on Ritchie and Delphis Lake. Management restricts fishing to fly-fishing only, without live bait.

Other summer pastimes include on-site tennis courts, and golf at the Pinestone Resort's eighteen-hole course, located twenty minutes away. The Domain property is grand for summer hikes, and mountain bikers may use the trails or the quiet backroads (some mountain bikes are available to guests).

The Domain remains open during the winter, and, with festoons of icicles on the cabins, and fresh snow falling almost daily, it is most photogenic. There are 28 kilometres of cross-country ski trails, and the inn provides a map. Some skiers believe that the Domain provides the best back-country skiing in the province, while others are partial to the 160-kilometre network of public trails that run throughout the Haliburton region. Downhill skiers head for Sir Sam's Ski Area, which is a short drive away. The inn has a small selection of snowshoes, skis and boots for guest use, and skaters can try their legs on the natural ice rink just outside the inn's front entrance.

One of the most adventurous endeavours for guests at the Domain is to spend a day at the cabin at Delphis lake, as part of a hiking or cross-country ski trek. The fully winterized cabin is equipped with a stove, and firewood is provided.

The Domain of Killien combines the atmosphere and fine dining of a five-star European hotel within thousands of hectares of granite, pine and lakes. If you are willing to suspend belief for just one brief visit, you will come away with a taste of paradise.

Domain of Killien

Box 810
Haliburton, ON
K0M 1S0
(705) 457-1100
Fax: (705) 457-3853
Innkeeper: Jean-Edouard Larcade

14 rooms and cottages
Dining room open to the public
Directions: From the village of Haliburton, drive west on County road 19 to Carroll Road. The Domain is on Carroll Road.
Tariffs: expensive
On site: hiking, sailing, canoeing, swimming, tennis, fly-fishing, cross-country skiing, skating
Off site: cycling and mountain biking, downhill skiing

THE VICTORIA INN

Gores Landing

Rice Lake country has the rural charm that warms the hearts of travellers — rolling hills dotted with red barns and white churches, tidy hamlets clustered around crossroads stores, wide stretches of pine forest, and fishing boats bobbing in the sunlight. The Victoria Inn is well situated for travellers wanting to tour this countryside, and innkeeper Donna Cane is a fount of information and ideas that can make your Rice Lake journey a memorable one.

Victoria Inn is located in Gores Landing, on the southern shore of Rice Lake. During the early days of the province, settlers travelled to the village from Port Hope by stagecoach, and then boarded a steamship bound for Ontario's interior. Today, Gores Landing is a community of gracious clapboard summer homes.

The inn, located just east of the village general store, was designed in the eastern seaboard style, with dormer windows, a golden cedar-shake exterior, a corner turret, and spacious lawns and gardens. It was built in 1902 as the "Willows," the summer home of painter Gerald Hayward. In the years before photography, portraits painted on ivory were highly valued, and Hayward established a reputation as Canada's premier practitioner of the craft, producing commissioned works for Edward VII, the czar and czarina of Russia, and various political leaders.

The Victoria Inn has as its mandate the provision of an atmosphere conducive to physical and emotional well-being. It achieves this through wholesome food, quiet surroundings, and a program of on-site events and off-site activities that showcase music and the arts.

The decor of the inn is simple, but fresh and bright. The wrap-around balcony of the original home has been converted into a bright, cheery dining room, decorated in crisp green, pink, and coordinating florals. The view of Rice Lake from the dining room windows is superb any time of day, but is especially beautiful at sunset. Just next to the dining room is the guest lounge area, which is oriented around the stone hearth and has a supply of reading material and information on local attractions.

The Victoria Inn menu is derived from a natural foods approach, and Donna Cane has worked hard to organize a network of local farmers to supply the inn with free-range chicken, lamb, goat cheese and fresh produce. These suppliers are listed on the back page of the inn menu. Because of commitment to healthy food, you will not see huge portions, heavy sauces, or highly spiced dishes in the dining room. What you will see are a pleasing variety of garden-fresh, organically grown vegetables and herbs, and lightly grilled local trout, pheasant, beef and lamb. The kitchen is also willing to work around special dietary requirements.

Appetizers include a fresh soup and several salads (green, Caesar, and a bean and grain combination). The list of entrees always includes the inn's signature fillet of trout steamed over pine needles and drizzled with lemon butter; chocolate chicken (simmered with mushrooms and Bailey's); and a pasta of the day. Desserts include fresh fruit pie, Black Forest cake and sorbets. Christmas and New Year's dinners, and other seasonal dinner events, always feature traditional festive foods, as well as vegetarian dishes. Donna Cane's interest in local and aboriginal foods is evidenced in the Thanksgiving menu of trout chowder, Indian corn salad, roast turkey with wild rice and fennel stuffing, and cranberry cheesecake.

The Victoria Inn has nine guest rooms, which are as spacious as you'll find anywhere. Some rooms, with three beds, are large enough to accommodate families. The guest rooms are decorated in the same colour scheme as the dining room, and all of the rooms have either a fireplace or a view of the lake. For a romantic, private retreat, reserve the turret room, which has a high, octagonal ceiling ornately panelled in wood. Interspersed with the rooms are nifty little nooks with window seats, perfect for curling up with the latest bestseller.

The Victoria Inn property is on the shore of Rice Lake, and the inn has its own dock. Boat rentals abound in the area for those who wish to fish or sail on their own. The inn can also arrange for a pontoon boat to pick up small groups for guided tours.

No innkeeper can match Donna Cane's familiarity with tourist resources in her region, or her ability to put together interesting day excursions for her guests. Is there a particular china pattern you are collecting? Need some milk paint for a refinishing project, or just love authentic antique folk art? Then let your host put together an antique hunting tour for you. Port Hope, Cobourg and Northumberland County are hot spots for antiques, and your host can advise you on the specialty of each shop.

Another interesting alternative for a day is to tour the countryside by visiting several excellent gardens (as ever, Donna Cane is a fountain of knowledge on the best ones). Well-known Schoolhouse Gardens is near Warkworth, and comprises one and a half hectares of walkways through beds of organically grown perennials, herbs, vegetables, and fruit and ornamental trees. Maple syrup from the property's own sugar bush is sold in the gift shop.

Rice Lake has attracted artists, musicians and writers for centuries, including the celebrated Catherine Parr Traill. It's natural, then, that the Victoria Inn is at the very centre of a lively arts community. Donna Cane is the president of an artisan's cooperative (which represents about one hundred individuals in the region), and can put together an individual or group studio tour. These tours are a great way to avoid the hassle and high cost of city art shopping and enjoy some country scenery at the same time. The inn is also the site of an annual art show and sale.

Music is celebrated at Victoria Inn through several special events. Labour Day features a jazz weekend, in which guests not only enjoy music (and a Texas barbecue), but can watch as specially invited visual artists sketch and paint the jazz musicians while they play. Other special events include antique car shows, poetry readings and other literary events, and art workshops.

Another cultural attraction is the 4th Line Theatre. Drama and comedy, with an emphasis on Ontario's history, is presented in a unique outdoor setting on the Winslow Farm. The farm is located on the 4th line, just south of Millbrook, a small community that is creating a large reputation for itself based on the high quality of work exhibited in the Millbrook Gallery.

Sports enthusiasts will also enjoy a trip to Victoria Inn, with its nearby golf courses, harness racing tracks, bowling lanes, curling rinks and cross-country ski trails. A popular pastime in the area is cycling, and the Inn can supply an excellent route map, complete with directions, level of difficulty, and length, for several routes.

Mountain biking is possible at the Ganaraska Forest, a huge expanse of hills and pine forest located a short distance from the inn. This same forest preserve offers a wide variety of cross-country ski trails and snowshoeing opportunities during the winter.

A tour of two historic sites — Serpent Mounds Provincial Park and Lang Pioneer Village — can make for a memorable day. Serpent Mounds Provincial Park was established to interpret and protect burial mounds left by nomadic tribes — referred to as Point Peninsula people — that visited this site annually between 2,000 and 1,600 years ago. The park interpretive centre displays the results of archaeological digs in the burial mounds and nearby middens, or garbage heaps. Results indicate that travelling groups came to harvest turtles, clams and wild rice from the lake, and that they were part of a continental trade network, perhaps exchanging turtleshell pottery for such items as silver and seashells. The mounds are situated on top of a small, steep-sided hill that offers an incredible view of Rice lake; there are eight oval mounds and one long, curvy one. The climb up the hill is worth it, not only to see the mounds, but also for the mystical feeling you get standing on the very vantage point enjoyed by these earlier visitors.

It would be hard to name a community more vibrant and vital than Lang Pioneer Village, located just north of Serpent Mounds. It is truly a working settlement, for any day you visit there are folks conducting the business of an early Ontario town: mending split-rail fences; dying wool in a steaming, black cauldron; hammering out hymns on the church pump-organ. The highlight of the village is the photogenic stone mill, which began producing stone-ground flour a century and a half ago and continues to do so today. There are dozens of other interesting buildings in the village, among them modest Fife cabin, furnished to the 1825 period, and the more comfortable Milburn House, restored to the 1870s. A print shop, hotel, blacksmith shop and cider barn are just a few of the commercial enterprises in town. Don't leave without making a purchase of village-made wool, tin cookie cutters or candles from the Menie General Store.

Rice Lake country has many country roads to delight the leisure driver. From Keene, drive west along County Road 2 to Highway 28; then drive south to the intersection with County

Road 9. In either direction, Road 9 offers long hills, wide vistas, and little traffic. West of this intersection is a very scenic stretch of highway that leads to Garden Hill, a small group of houses clustered around a general store. The community is a mere shadow of its former self, which boasted no less than eight mills along its babbling brook. East of the intersection with Highway 28, Road 9 leads to Bewdley, the self-named gateway to Rice Lake. In Bewdley, the town docks are busy with several boat-rental operations, and there is always some lucky angler bringing in a good-sized fish, and several others lined up on the dock, eager to hear the replay.

Whether you come for a healthy, active retreat, or just plan to occupy a lounge chair and take in the view, you'll find that The Victoria Inn is a most satisfying discovery.

The Victoria Inn

Gores Landing, ON
K0K 2E0
(905) 342-3261
Fax: (905) 342-2798
Innkeepers: Donna and Donald Cane

9 rooms
Dining room open to public
Directions: Exit 472 northbound off Highway 401. Drive north on County Road 18 to Gores Landing. Turn right to the inn.
Tariffs: inexpensive
On site: outdoor swimming pool
Off site: 4th Line Theatre, Serpent Mounds Provincial Park, Lang Pioneer Village, gardens, shopping, antique hunting, harness racing, pontoon-boat cruises, country drives, golf, boating, fishing, kayaking, canoeing, windsurfing, cycling and mountain biking, cross-country skiing

WOODLAWN TERRACE INN

Cobourg

From the time of early settlement, Cobourg's civic founders were intent on creating a city of importance. Where nature failed to provide a harbour, they created breakwaters and piers; when they were competing with Toronto and Kingston in a bid to have their town named capital of Upper Canada, they erected stately Victoria Hall. One of those ambitious local citizens was United Empire Loyalist Ebenezer Perry, who resided in an imposing mansion on Division Street. That mansion is now the Woodlawn Terrace Inn, which makes an appropriate home for those who travel to Cobourg to take in its historic sites and the region's many antique shops.

The Woodlawn Terrace Inn, constructed during the mid 1830s, is a classic example of Regency architecture, which was favoured by the Loyalists, and can be seen in many towns along the north shore of Lake Ontario. Innkeeper Gerda Della-Casa retained the character of the building while upgrading the interior to provide contemporary hotel accommodations and a popular restaurant.

The Woodlawn is a two-storey brick home with a hip roof, a white columned porch and a second-storey balcony. The Wood-lawn's respectable appearance is accented by hanging baskets of flowers, large trees and colourful flowerbeds inside a circular driveway. A walk around the property reveals a myriad of architectural detailing that is a rich feast for the eyes, including twenty-four paned windows with black shutters, elaborate wrought-iron railings along the porches, and classic ornamentation under each eave. Gerda Della-Casa loves to point out that those windows are original to the house, evidenced by the initials of Ebenezer Perry's son, which he scratched into the glass on his twenty-first birthday — as the story goes.

There are fourteen rooms in the inn, twelve in an addition, and two in the original home. These two — the Presidential Suite and the Honeymoon suite — are luxuriously appointed, spacious rooms with four-poster beds, fireplaces and whirlpool baths. The decor features balloon valances over the windows, deep woodwork, and vases of fresh flowers and plants. The rooms in the addition are more modern, but they are also spacious, and feature antiques and reproduction furnishings and balconies or patios.

The Della-Casa family, like all good innkeepers, have brought the influence of their own heritage and character to the property. The inn's interior has a European feel, with furnishings imported from Italy. The heart of the inn is the lounge area, which is arranged around a remarkable curved front bar of inlaid rosewood that was created in Florence. Other furnishings include deeply upholstered brown leather armchairs, and striped sofas. Adjoining the lounge are two dining areas: the main room, decorated in rose and green and coordinating florals, and a very private back garden with patio tables and chairs.

The menu also reflects a European atmosphere. Bruschetta is a popular starter, as is a salad of Bocconcini mozzarella with tomato and pesto. A highly recommended first course is a superb roast carrot and lobster bisque accented with ginger. The Woodlawn prides itself on its high-quality fruits de mer, which include pasta with salmon or swordfish, and shrimp, and scallops Sambucca flambéed at your table. Veal is also a house specialty, and it is served grilled with lemon and caper sauce, or with mozzarella and parmesan topping.

Stephen Della-Casa is the inn's sommelier, and his list focuses on the wines of Europe and California. The inn holds wine-tasting seminars, and there are frequent special dinners organized around regional cuisine and wines.

The Woodlawn Terrace Inn's midweek luncheon buffets are reasonably priced, which makes it a sought-out restaurant for business meetings. The inn's fully equipped meeting rooms can also be booked for small conferences. Conference planners appreciate the inn's smaller size, which means that they can book the entire facility, and thus ensure privacy.

Both Port Hope and Cobourg were settled by United Empire
• Loyalists who quickly established stable communities in which business flourished. To this day, both towns are magnets for antique hunters. Cobourg began as a lakeside port; its commodious harbour was constructed almost a century and a half ago. Shipping and shipbuilding were important early industries. To this day, the town remains a popular haven for recreational boaters on the

Great Lakes. Plan on a half a day to wander along the piers, watch the gulls soar on the lake breezes, and hear the snap of canvas as sailors head out for adventure. Be sure to visit beloved Victoria Park, which has a long white-sand beach and a bandshell for summertime concerts.

Majestic Victoria Hall dominates the main street of town. This Palladian building of grey sandstone block was designed by American Kivas Tully to express the city fathers' hope that their town would become the economic and political heart of the country. Huge columns, pediments, a speaker's balcony, and ornate imperial stone carvings decorate the building's front face, and the roof is crowned with a cupola and clock tower. Victoria Hall may be at its best during the Christmas season, when the civic square in front of the building is decorated with green garlands.

Stepping through Victoria Hall's huge black doors is like stepping back a century in time, for very little of the interior has changed. The floor is a black-and-white-stone checkerboard, and twin grand staircases are located at each side of the foyer. A sunken courtroom, closely modelled after the Old Bailey, in London, is the centrepiece of the main floor. It is used as a court on Mondays and Thursdays, but you can survey the austere room, with its original woodwork, flooring and decor, on all other weekdays. Also on the main floor is the office of Father of Confederation James Cockburn (ask the guard for a view), which has been decorated to appear as it would have in the nineteenth century.

The pièce de résistance of Victoria Hall is the breathtaking Grand Concert Hall. The high ceilings are covered with trompel'oeil paintings that appear to be ornate plasterwork. The hall is the site of many civic and private functions, and is the venue for a full winter season of professional music and theatre (the Woodlawn Terrace staff can arrange for tickets). Upstairs from the ballroom is the Art Gallery of Northumberland, which holds changing exhibits of works from local and national artists. Victoria Square, located behind the hall, is the site of the Cobourg Farmers Market, which convenes each Saturday morning from May to October.

A dramatic change of pace awaits just down the street from Victoria Hall at a tiny Regency cottage, now occupied by the Chamber of Commerce. At one time, this was the childhood home of early Hollywood superstar Marie Dressler. There is hardly a more picturesque home in the province: a single-storey red-brick house with a hip roof, shuttered windows and a front door with sidelights. The Chamber of Commerce lovingly preserved Dressler's memory in several rooms of exhibits, which include photographs, a mock-up of the set from the movie *Min and Bill*, and a video biography of Dressler. The Chamber office is a good place to pick up a walking tour brochure that describes Cobourg's historic buildings, or a guide to the many antique shops located in Northumberland County.

One of the densest concentrations of antique and art stores is in neighbouring Port Hope, a small, charming town built along the steep valley of the Ganaraska River. There are many stores to investigate in Port Hope, but they are located within a few blocks of one another, so you can park the car and spend the day on foot. While not all stores can be listed, the following are a small sample to whet the appetite.

Near the top of the hill, on Walton Street, is the Owl & the Pussycat, which sells wooden chests and harvest tables, as well as locally produced pottery. The shop has a tearoom with a view over the downtown. Further downhill is the Linton Shaw Gallery, which has a fine exhibit of original works in metal, glass, clay, watercolour and acrylic. Right across the street is one of the highlights of Port Hope, Lord Russborough's Annex, the place to go if you have a hankering for historic Canadian and European maps and prints. Chatwood & Simmons is chock-full of Victoriana: china, silverware, lace table linens, and a delightful selection of antique jewellery in amber and silver. The largest collection of antiques in the area is in the three-storey Smith's Creek Antiques. Here there are huge armoires and sleighs, rocking horses and paintings, as well as smaller items. Antique Associates houses the collections of three dealers, and they all specialize in unique and rare items from across the centuries; there is surely a conversation piece for every home here.

Wander down Queen Street to Estate Treasures, which is like grandma's china buffet multiplied many times over. John Street also shouldn't be overlooked. Bargain hunters and rummage-sale fans will love the Picker's Market, with a typical assortment of antiques, used furniture and collectibles. For lunch, head for the Carlyle Inn, which is housed in the 1857 Bank of Upper Canada building. Another fine eatery is the Beamish Pub, where pub grub is served in the 1848 home and shop of Port Hope's first shoemaker.

Gerda Della-Casa is well prepared to help guests plan a day out of town. The inn can arrange for tee times at several local golf courses, and can book fishing charters for those who wish to try their luck at landing a Lake Ontario salmon. Bike rentals are available in Cobourg for guests to explore the country byways in a leisurely fashion. During the winter, head for the Northumberland Forest. This huge tract of hilly forest has many groomed and marked cross-country ski trails for skiers of any ability. The innkeepers can also help arrange for snowmobile rentals and provide information on local snowmobile trails.

Cobourg is a terrific spot to escape the city crowds for a few days of pampering and leisurely daytripping. There are outdoor activities and antique shops galore, and the Woodlawn Terrace Inn provides an atmosphere of continental grace and restfulness that will enhance any holiday.

Woodlawn Terrace Inn

420 Division Street
Cobourg, ON
K9A 3R9
(905) 372-2235
Fax: (905) 372-4673
Innkeepers: Gerda and Domenico Della-Casa

14 rooms
Dining room open to public
Directions: Exit 474 on the 401 is Division Street; follow it to the inn.
Tariffs: inexpensive
On site: garden
Off site: Victoria Hall, Dressler House, antique hunting, farmers market, golf, fishing, boating

STE. ANNE'S
COUNTRY INN & SPA

Grafton

What do you get when you combine an unusual stone country house and an innkeeper dedicated to providing a healing atmosphere for guests? Ste. Anne's, the product of just such a union, offers guests an experience unrivalled in Ontario.

It takes just a few moments of repose in the inn's main lounge to realize that you are in an exceptional place. All good inns provide quiet, but St. Anne's quiet is a soul-deep sense of peace and renewal. And while a day away should offer a break from your humdrum routine, a Ste. Anne's day will reawaken your inner enthusiasm.

The core of the inn and spa is a solid stone farmhouse constructed in 1857 for Samuel Massey of the Canadian establishment family. In 1939, the estate was purchased by the Blaffer family, who, like many well-to-do Americans, spent their summers in the Cobourg area. The Blaffer family made many alterations to the house, such as the large east addition and walled courtyard. The irregular facade, turret, and broad archway of the fieldstone house fit the common image of a Tudor castle.

The architecture is surpassed only by the setting. Ste. Anne's is located well off the beaten track, among the rolling hills of Northumberland County. The house is long and low, and rambles along the crest of a hill. The view from any part of the home is immense, a panorama dominated by the glistening waters of Lake Ontario. Far below are green fields and hedgerows, and although highways and towns are located between the inn and the lake, they are tucked away in valleys and hidden by trees, so that one has a sense of being able to reach out and touch the water. Arriving guests never fail to gasp when they see vivid blue horizon framed by the stone archway that connects the original house to the east wing.

The Corcoran family took over the house in 1981, and they performed a great deal of repair and renovation work. The house is so naturally suited to hospitality that the Corcoran's began a bed-and-breakfast operation, which gradually increased in scale. Jim Corcoran took over the helm and gradually introduced spa services, such as facials and massage, under the guidance of Toronto spa-owner Ray Civello. Those simple initial services have progressed to the point where Ste. Anne's is now considered the premiere spa in the province. The focus of treatment and activity at Ste. Anne's is always more on inner well-being and outer radiance than on conventional cosmetic treatments.

Ste. Anne's spa offers a wide diversity of treatments. The following is just a sample to pique your curiosity. "Body Work" refers to a variety of massage techniques that include Swedish and Shiatsu massage, reflexology, aromatherapy, Japanese Reiki therapy, scalp massage and dry-brush massage. The latter involves a brushing to remove old skin, a steam in the sauna, and an application of moisturizers.

Hydrotherapy is popular at Ste. Anne's, and all therapies utilize the site's own natural spring water. The Moor mud bath begins with a hot-tub soak and a shower followed by a ten-minute immersion in a deeply relaxing warm mud tub, which is followed by a final cleansing shower. The ultimate treatment combines the mud bath with either a sea-salt glow scrub and an invigorating high-pressure shower, or with a body polish, in which, after exfoliation treatment, the body is washed with a warm-water brush and treated to a power shower. A full range of facials, manicures, and pedicures is also provided at Ste. Anne's. Aveda products are used throughout the spa, and they are also for sale at the inn shop.

A typical spa day begins with a short fitness class that takes place in one of the most pleasant rooms in the inn. Natural light pours in through picture windows that face the lake, fresh breezes carry the fragrance of the meadows, and there's plenty of room for everyone to stretch out. The classes include stretches, light aerobics, meditation and visual imagery. Fitness consultations with personal trainers may include strength and flexibility testing, exercise programs, and discussion of personal presentation.

Other organized exercise activities include guided fitness walks over Ste. Anne's 250 hectares of meadows and woodlands. There are tennis courts and a swimming pool on site for individual workouts. The pool contains the same spring water used in the spa, which means that very little chlorine is necessary — a pleasant change from most hotel pools. The inn's exercise room contains a treadmill, weight machines and other workout gear. The hot tub has its own secluded nook with a private view over the grounds, and there is also a steam sauna.

Ste. Anne's packaged getaways include meals, accommodation and spa treatments. Their popular "Stress Express" is a one-day breakaway that includes rail transport from Toronto or Kingston to Cobourg, limousine service from the station to the spa, and a day's worth of treatment. Guests are pampered and rejuvenated, and then sent home on the train at the end of the day. Each winter is celebrated with a program called "The Twelve Weeks of Winter." In this program, every week has a special theme — watercolour painting, meditation, or yoga, for example — with instructors in the specialty field on site daily.

Ste. Anne's has a variety of accommodation styles. The inn proper has seven pleasant, individually decorated rooms. Each room is a delight, decorated with an eclectic array of antiques and unusual accents that are family heirlooms or have been collected on travels. These furnishings, together with lovely choices in fabrics, and a fireplace, create a familiar, comfortable ambience. The inn also has three spacious luxury suites, which feature cathedral ceilings, fireplaces and whirlpool tubs.

The inn also has guest rooms in five nearby cottages (renovated farmhouses), which are well suited for small groups. Each cottage has a living room, a self-contained kitchen, and sleeping space for several people. Guests at the cottages may eat at the inn and partake in all spa activities.

The inn has a common living room, where guests can mingle, read, or play a quiet game. The room has been recently redecorated to return it to its original sunny yellow colour scheme, which suits an inn devoted to "bringing out the sun that exists in the heart of every person." Throughout the building, guests are at ease wearing their inn housecoats — the practical way to dress between spa sessions.

Meals at Ste. Anne's are designed to be healthy, but are definitely not boring. Chef Aram Sailliam, a graduate of George Brown College, creates meals that rival those of any big city restaurant, and vegetarian and light choices are available at every meal. The inn makes its own pasta, soup and baked goods, and inn-made bread, jam and salad dressings are sold to the public. Herbs and vegetables are organically grown in season.

A typical meal may begin with carrot and rosemary soup or a salad of mixed greens and goat's cheese. Popular entrees include chicken stuffed with duck, sun-dried tomatoes, brie and mushrooms; baked rainbow trout served with a shrimp and mushroom sauté; and a grilled pork tenderloin brochette with red-wine demiglaze. Cast all thoughts of restraint aside for dessert — profiterole swans filled with Chantilly cream and served with a strawberry coulis, or chocolate raspberry torte made with fine Belgian chocolate and glazed with brandy. Ste. Anne's breakfast offers a good choice of eggs, hot cereals, müsli or yogurt with fruit, or a changing chef's special that is always worth waking up for.

While most guests spend their entire time at the inn, there are several other ways to enjoy the Northumberland countryside. The inn provides bikes for guest use, and local roadways are fairly clear of traffic. Mountain bikers can head for the Northumberland Forest for a true off-road challenge.

A very pleasant daytrip can be spent in Grafton, on Lake Ontario just south of Ste. Anne's. This United Empire Loyalist village is very old by Ontario standards, and many of its Regency and Georgian homes and commercial buildings have been carefully preserved. One of these, the Barnum House Museum (1819), is open to the public. Costumed interpreters provide informative tours that point out many unique furnishings, such as a magic lantern, a precursor of the stereoscope, and two precious musical instruments: a clavichord and a dulcimer. Grafton is also well known for its wonderful antique stores.

Guests who wish to travel a little farther afield will want to take in the natural beauty of Presqu'ile Provincial Park, a sandy spit of land that juts out into Lake Ontario near Brighton. Presqu'ile is a favourite haunt of naturalists because of its diversity of habitat (marsh, beaches, maple-beech forest and cedar forest), which attracts a corresponding diversity of animal life. Presqu'ile is best known for its spectacular autumn bird migrations. Beginning with shorebirds in August and ending with birds of prey in November, there's always an impressive show to see. Monarchs butterflies also make use of Presqu'ile's position as the most southerly point on the lakeshore, congregating on trees and shrubs until weather conditions are best for the long and hazardous crossing of the lake.

The lighthouse at the tip of the park's peninsula is the second oldest still in operation on the Great Lakes, and a new marine heritage centre is located in the lighthouse keeper's cottage. Here you can find out about the opportunities to participate in butterfly banding, stargazing, waterfowl viewing and other events organized by park staff. The centre also has interesting exhibits on the human history of the peninsula, which includes rum smuggling, piracy, and shipwrecks. After a day of swimming on Presqu'ile's beach or following warblers through the woodlands, you will be ready for more pampering at your home base.

In the minds of many Ontarians, Ste. Anne's Country Inn & Spa has become synonymous with stress relief. But don't wait until life seems out of balance to begin indulging yourself — make Ste. Anne's a regular part of your routine, and relish the difference it can make.

Ste. Anne's Country Inn & Spa

R.R. 1
Grafton, ON
K0K 2G0
(905) 349-2493
1-800-263-2663
Fax: (905) 349-3531
Innkeeper: Jim Corcoran

12 rooms
Dining room not open to public
Not licensed, but you are welcome to bring your own
Directions: Exit at 487 on 401, drive north to Academy Hill
    Road and follow signs.
Tariffs: expensive
On site: full spa facilities, walking, outdoor pool, tennis
Off site: antique hunting, Presqu'ile Provincial Park, beaches,
    golf, cycling

AROWHON PINES

Algonquin Park

In the popular mind, the name Ontario is synonymous with images of rugged northern landscapes. Mica and quartz glistening in pink granite, the unearthly call of a loon, the soft cushion of a pine-needle carpet underfoot. There's no place in the province more closely associated with our tremendous natural splendour than Algonquin Provincial Park, partly because of its proximity to the populous regions of the province, but also because the services of park staff and private outfitters enable everyone, regardless of back-country experience or fitness level, to make contact with real wilderness in some way.

Arowhon Pines has played host to a loyal clientele through six decades. The lodge has a choice site on the shore of Little Joe Lake, 8 kilometres off Highway 60, the busy corridor that traverses the park's southwest quadrant. Arowhon Pines is close enough to civilization that guests may take part in the full range of park services, such as guided hikes and paddle trips, but far enough away from the activity to be in its own wooded world.

Arowhon's story begins at the height of the Depression, when remarkable Lillian Kates — an Algonquin legend in her own right — began what was to become one of Ontario's best-known children's summer camps. Visiting parents and siblings required accommodation, and so Kates leased land a few kilometres away on Little Joe Lake at what would be the site of Arowhon Pines. The inn was built using local talent and local materials. All of Arowhon's buildings were constructed from the site's own trees, which were cut, shaped and put into place over a two-year period by brothers Paul and Jack Lucasavitch. The inn's pièce de résistance is a hexagonal dining room that sweeps out over the water. At its centre is a stone fireplace with a steel chimney that rises about 10 metres to a hexagonal cupola. One of the most evocative and familiar portraits of our province is a photograph of Arowhon's stone-and-log dining room, with its expansive red-shingle roof, shimmering Lake Joe, and a backdrop of green pine and puffy white clouds.

The dining room is not only the visual focal point of Arowhon, it is also the very heart and soul of the resort. Helen and Eugene Kates (son and daughter-in-law of Lillian) enjoy a tremendously loyal clientele, which has been built on Helen's exacting, unwavering standards in kitchen management, and Eugene's commitment to warm, caring service. Although Helen's natural instincts for kitchen arts (her father was a professional chef) have been honed to a keen edge through years of experience, she does not rest on her laurels but consistently strives for even greater perfection each season. A case in point: every work station in the kitchen has a computer terminal loaded with Helen's six hundred recipes, and every worker follows the screen's instructions to the letter, which ensures perfect consistency from meal to meal. Head chef Andreas Babinski was trained in Europe and gained experience on luxury cruise ships. He produces an extraordinary dining experience three meals a day, seven days a week, guaranteed. Like all of Arowhon's workers, the dining-room staff are at the top of their trade — but don't try to tip; acceptance of a gratuity results in immediate dismissal!

Each meal at Arowhon has an interesting medley of items to choose from, and guests are welcome to request second helpings or small portions of a combination of several dishes. Breakfast provides the fuel necessary for canoe and hike treks; there are fruit compotes, hot and cold cereals, cheese and cold-meat platters, eggs served any style, grilled kippers, and French toast made with Arowhon Pines' own raisin challah. Lunch provides soup, salads, and a choice of creative main courses including cornmeal pizza with grilled vegetables and pork schnitzel, with Lyonnaise potatoes and Bavarian red cabbage.

Dinner guests begin with appetizers set out on two pine harvest tables. There is always a warm item, such as spicy chicken wings or sausage rolls, and a house salad with dressing. Terrines and pâtés (chicken liver, duck, trout) are served with chutney and homemade Melba toast. Specialty salads include a grilled and marinated vegetable salad with mushrooms, peppers, eggplant or leeks, and salads based on millet, wild rice and couscous.

Table service begins with soups — clam, mussel and sweet corn chowder, or chilled yogurt-cucumber — served with the inn's freshly baked breads, which include rosemary-flavoured foccaccio and buttermilk biscuits. A long list of entrees includes Singapore-style grouper, maple-glazed ham, and Ontario's best prime rib, perfectly prepared and thinly sliced. Of course, Helen

Kates and her staff don't stop there. After dinner, guests are invited to another harvest table with an ever-changing tableau of sweets: cream pies, fruit pies, frozen ice-cream bombes, fresh fruit and cheese, warm fruit crumble with vanilla custard (much recommended), trifle, mousse, squares and cookies. The perfect way to end your meal is to take your tea or coffee to the wrap-around porch and watch the loons perform an evening sailpast.

Arowhon's forty-nine guest rooms are located in several cabins. There are three private cabins, several with two to four bedrooms clustered around a common living room (great for families), and other buildings with as many as twelve bedrooms. The rooms all have ensuite baths (and bathrobes). The buildings have welcoming central living rooms with ceiling-high stone fireplaces, lots of comfy couches, a good supply of reading material, and a fridge for storing wine and other bar supplies (Arowhon is not licensed, so bring your own). The guest bedrooms are decorated very sparely, which might be a disappointment in other settings but seems appropriate for Arowhon's wilderness environment. Each cabin has a porch with Muskoka chairs, perfect for enjoying the coffee, tea, lemonade and cookies that are always available between meals.

The best way to spend time in serene Algonquin is in quiet contemplation, whether at the lodge or out in the park, and Arowhon provides all the right equipment, free of charge, to enable you to find your own piece of tranquillity. Take advantage of Arowhon's packed knapsack lunches of sandwiches and a hot or cold thermos; these should be ordered the day before your trek.

Your hosts also provide a full supply of canoes, paddles, life jackets and maps. Little Joe Lake is connected to a long canoe route through several lakes, so it is possible to experience different scenery every day of your stay. (Be sure to consult *Exploring Algonquin Park,* by Joanne Kates, who, as manager of Arowhon Camp, is as familiar as anyone with canoe routes and hiking trails.) Arowhon staff can put guests in contact with guides for canoe trips, fishing trips or hikes.

The dock area is the place to try your hand with the inn's three sailboats, kayaks and windsurfers. Lake swimming is a part of any northern holiday, and the dock, diving platform and floating raft add to the fun. A games building with bumper pool, table tennis, puzzles and board games is also located on site, and movies are shown each evening. Outdoor on-site activities include tennis, badminton and shuffleboard. A full day of exercise may be followed by some time in the sauna (let the staff know ahead of time and they will stoke up the fire for you).

Algonquin Park is known for its well-maintained and marked trails, each of which has a corresponding interpretive brochure available at the park entrance. The 11-kilometre Mizzy Lake trail, which traverses the shores of nine different lakes, is recommended for photos of Algonquin's famous moose, bear, loons and martens. Good views of the park's undulating hills — a dazzling tapestry of green, red and orange in autumn — can be had from the Hardwood Lookout and the Lookout Trail. Centennial Ridges is a demanding day-long hike that also provides superb high-altitude viewpoints. Other trails introduce hikers to northern ecology: Bat Lake (an acidic lake), Spruce Bog Boardwalk, Beaver Pond, and Whiskey Rapid. There are several marked trails on Arowhon's own property, one of which meets up with the Mizzy Lake trail, making it an excellent all-day adventure.

For exhilarating off-road fun, mountain bikers may bike on Algonquin's Minnesing trail (loops of 4.7, 10, 17 and 23 kilometres), or along the abandoned railway line that runs through Arowhon's own property.

Many people visit Algonquin Park for its less rigorous charms. The park staff are justifiably proud of the impressive visitor centre built to celebrate Algonquin's centenary, in 1993. The theme of the centre is Algonquin past and present. Historic documents, interactive computer games and meticulously detailed dioramas of forest and lake scenes tell the story of a billion years of geologic history, a few thousand years of aboriginal settlement, and a few decades of logging and resort development. An excellent narrated slide show makes the point that what took mother nature one billion years to create took man only a lifetime to alter forever. The visitor centre has a well-stocked book shop, cafeteria, and a daily wildlife sightings board. Another park museum, the Algonquin Logging Museum, is located at Algonquin's eastern entrance. It features an audio-visual display on logging, a 1-kilometre trail with displays of logging equipment, a camboose shed that was home to fifty loggers each winter, and a blacksmith shop (horses were used in the logging industry until the 1950s).

Eugene and Helen Kates run an extraordinary hostelry in one of the nation's most enchanting settings. A stay at Arowhon allows fortunate guests to do three important things in one holiday: explore Northern Ontario's wildlands, savour the products of a very effective kitchen, and luxuriate in the radiant warmth of good service.

Arowhon Pines

Algonquin Park, ON
P0A 1B0
(705) 633-5661
(705) 633-5662
Fax: (705) 633-5795
Winter address:
297 Balliol Street
Toronto, ON
M4S 1C7
(416) 483-4393
Fax: (416) 483-4429
Innkeepers: Eugene and Helen Kates
Open June through Thanksgiving

49 rooms
Dining room open to the public
Not licensed, but you are welcome to bring your own
Directions: The Arowhon Pines road is signposted on Highway 60, 15 kilometres inside the western entrance to Algonquin Park.
Tariffs: expensive
On site: tennis, badminton, sailing, swimming, canoeing, fishing, hiking
Off site: Algonquin Park Visitor Centre, Logging Museum, hiking, biking, canoeing and guided hikes and canoe trips

ROSEMOUNT
BED & BREAKFAST INN

Kingston

Good theatre, fine dining, historic architecture, interesting shops, unique museums, and some of the best sailing in North America. Kingston sounds like a holiday made in heaven. Many travellers are beginning to realize that Kingston has so much to offer that it can no longer be thought of as just a weekend destination.

Rosemount Bed & Breakfast Inn is a wonderful historic property located a few blocks from all the major attractions. A mansion built for dry-goods merchant Edward Hardy, in 1849, Rosemount is in the very heart of historic Kingston. The inn brochure captures so much in one photograph: an arched portico, its twin columns decorated with lamps held aloft by diminutive dragons; maroon eave brackets and cornices with classic detailing; and lush foliage and blooms in vases, planters and wall pots. The grounds are enclosed by a fine wrought-iron fence, with stone pillars at the gate, and similar wrought-iron work occurs in front of second-floor windows. The scene is almost Mediterranean, although wrought in local limestone. It is hard to imagine a more intriguing or historic setting for an inn.

Holly Doughty and John Edwards are Rosemount's innkeepers, and they restored the house to something resembling a single-family residence after its years as an apartment building. The parlour is a most pleasant room, with tall, narrow windows topped by leaded-glass transoms. Hinged inside shutters fold up into built-in cupboards when not in use; when extended, they keep the house shaded and cool — another nod to Mediterranean design. The room is decorated in soothing mauves, pinks and blues. An 1849 atlas of Frontenac and Lennox & Addington Counties rests on a stand, lacy doilies adorn the side tables, an ornate chess set stands at the ready.

There are eight guest rooms at Rosemount, and all but one has an ensuite bathroom. The high-ceilinged rooms are decorated with auction-sale treasures (Holly Doughty is a good one to consult if antiquing is your passion). The Tower Room is a special place, with a lofty sitting room and a balcony that surveys the entire neighbourhood — a terrific place to spend a summer's evening. The Rosemount room is located above the parlour, and has the same rounded window bay. It is very romantic, with rose and green floral wallpaper and matching draperies on the floor-to-ceiling windows. The carved, four-poster bed, with a vivid rose bedskirt, is so high that it comes with its own footstool. The bathroom has a pedestal sink and a convenient towel warmer. The Macdonald is a two-room suite with two beds and a daybed. It is decorated in cool blues, with striped wallpaper, yellow-and-blue comforters and white-and-blue oriental carpets over hardwood floors. The two-storey Coach House, a self-contained apartment, is a wonderful retreat for two, with skylights, pine floors, a loft bedroom and a whirlpool tub.

John Edwards is the chef for breakfast, which is truly a masterpiece of a meal. The menu changes daily, and consists of several courses. During the summer, fruit and vegetables are brought in from the market, and fresh herbs are taken from the garden. Breakfast pie, a lightly textured cottage-cheese pie with raspberry-and-red-currant glaze, is served with kiwi and orange slices and vanilla yogurt. That may be followed by the crab-and-Swiss-cheese frittata, with fresh herbs and new potatoes. Breakfast always includes a selection of gourmet breads, including multi-grain and rye, and excellent coffee and tea are always available on the sideboard. The dining room is furnished in style, with a gleaming table, Willow china and floral needlepoint cloths. The dining room overlooks the garden, which is full of bloom during the summer and busy with birds at the feeders during the winter.

The morning meal has two sittings, generally 7:30 and 8:30 during the week, and about an hour later on weekends. Doughty asks that guests, who sit together, take the time to introduce themselves. Before long, business cards are exchanged and friendships are formed. Weekday guests are often in Kingston on business trips, and they appreciate the chance to have a pleasant meal before starting their day. Weekend and holiday guests rave about Edward's morning feast as a good way to fuel up for an active day. For the remainder of the day the house is completely quiet, a perfect place to savour some downtime.

Rosemount recently added spa treatments to its list of guest services. With advance notice, aromatherapy and relaxation massage can be enjoyed in the Gazebo Room.

Rosemount is only a few blocks from the major sights in town, and is especially well located for taking in a play at the Grand Theatre. It is also close to two museums on the campus of Queen's University: the Agnes Etherington Art Centre and the Miller Museum of Geology and Mineralogy. Kingston also has museums devoted to hockey, woodworking, archaeology and military communications.

Venerable Fort Henry remains highly revered among residents and travellers. The immense grey fort is located just east of downtown, high atop a hill that provides a panoramic vista of the Royal Military College, the Kingston waterfront and the islands of the St. Lawrence River. At the fort you will witness the daily military manoeuvres performed by militia in period costume of red jacket and tall black hat. Cannons roar, boots smack the pavement, drummers keep time and a drill sergeant shouts out commands — exciting enough during the afternoon parade and drill, but an exceptional scene after dark when sparks and flashes from muskets and cannons light up the parade square.

Those who love historic buildings will want to spend a few days walking through the older section of Kingston. This city has the best collection of limestone churches, stores and grand homes west of Montreal, and Kingstonians lovingly refer to their historic buildings as "old stones." The City Hall is an impressive building with a columned portico and round dome with a four-sided clock tower. Across the street is a tourist information centre, where you can join up with conducted bike tours of town, or with the narrated trolley tours.

For almost two centuries, farmers have been selling their wares — fresh flowers, fruit, vegetables, cheese and crafts — in Market Square, immediately behind City Hall. The site is still a hub of activity on Tuesdays, Thursdays and Saturdays, and there's an antique market on Sundays. Some of Kingston's favourite emporiums are almost as old as the market, and many of them are located nearby on quaint Brock Street. Cooke's Old World Shop has been selling gourmet teas and coffees since 1865, and many patrons wouldn't shop anywhere else. The Kingston Gallery of Clocks has a full selection of glamorous timekeepers, from mantel-top models to grandfather clocks. The Doll Attic is stocked with collector's favourites, such as Anne of Green Gables and Madame Alexander dolls. There is also a complete line of doll houses and lavish costumes.

The history of life on the Great Lakes is brilliantly portrayed at the Marine Museum of the Great Lakes on Ontario Street. The museum is housed in an old shipyard established in 1790, and the dry-dock building is Ontario's oldest, opened in 1890 by Sir John A. Macdonald. Exhibits of photographs, maps, text, historic documents and ship's logs detail the history of navigation on the Great Lakes. There are dozens of models of lake freighters, navy vessels and pleasure craft, both historic and modern. Changing displays provide insight into shipwrecks, life aboard a freighter, and shipbuilding. The *Alexander Henry*, a 3,000-ton ice breaker is also part of the museum (docked at the wharf just outside), and with the help of a self-guiding brochure, you can explore the ship from stem to stern.

Unlike many modern cities, Kingston has treated its waterfront with care and respect. Many sailors have made the city home in order to take advantage of the challenging winds of Lake Ontario, and harbour boat cruises are a good way to capture photos of brilliantly coloured sails against the lake's wide horizon of vivid blue water and whitecaps. The tiny village of Portsmouth was once a town in its own right, but it was swallowed up by Kingston's westward expansion. Portsmouth Olympic Harbour is a busy marina where you can charter a yacht and skipper, or simply wander the piers and watch the boats go by. Many houses near the harbour, sporting nautical names and decorations, are now bed and breakfast establishments.

There is car-ferry service several times daily between Kingston and Wolfe Island. Although the ride to the island takes only a few minutes, the island community seems far removed from modern life. The scenery is wonderfully pastoral: wildflower-dotted meadows, pebbled coves that shelter small sailboats, isolated churches, and maple lined laneways that lead to stone farmsteads. The level roadways and lack of traffic make Wolfe Island ideal for cycling, and the ferry sometimes carries as many bikes as cars.

Kingston is proud to have been the home of Canadian founding father Sir John A. Macdonald — his name and accomplishments are ubiquitous here. Bellevue House, Macdonald's home for a brief span in the late 1840s, is open to the public and provides an insight into the great man's career, as well as an inside look at an Italianate home. A Bellevue visit begins with a film on local and national history, which is followed by a tour of the house, from cook's quarters to parlour. Gardeners will want to spend time on the spacious grounds, for not only are the flowers lovely, but they can also observe costumed gardeners employing nineteenth-century equipment and methods.

Because Rosemount is a bed and breakfast inn, dinner must be taken out, but that is not a problem in Kingston, because there are several good eateries downtown. Chez Piggy's is located in an old livery panelled in pine and butternut; choice summer seating is available in a courtyard surrounded by limestone buildings. The River Mill Restaurant, also a good choice for dinner, is elegantly housed in an 1880 cotton mill, with large picture windows looking over the Cataraqui River.

Travellers who want to take in Kingston's premier attractions may want to take advantage of Rosemount's Magical History Tour, which is available to guests who stay for a minimum of two nights. Although the activities in this specially priced package vary somewhat according to season, they usually include a tour of Fort Henry's museums, a visit to Bellevue House, an excursion on the Kingston tour trolley, and dinner certificates to popular downtown restaurants. During the summer, the package includes tickets to a performance at the Grand Theatre, and a dinner cruise aboard the *Island Belle*, which departs from Kingston for a performance at the Thousand Island Playhouse, in Gananoque, and returns later in the evening.

The convenient location, familial atmosphere and outstanding breakfast offered at Rosemount Bed & Breakfast Inn make it a choice destination for anyone bound for historic Kingston.

Rosemount Bed & Breakfast Inn

46 Sydenham Street South
Kingston, ON
K7L 3H1
(613) 531-8844
Fax: (613) 531-9722
Innkeepers: Holly Doughty and John Edwards

8 rooms
Bed and breakfast only
Directions: Exit 615 south off 401; turn left on Johnson Street,
    then right on Sydenham Street.
Tariffs: moderate
On site: garden
Off site: Grand Theatre, Marine Museum of the Great Lakes,
    Wolfe Island, Old Fort Henry, sightseeing tours, boat
    cruises, sailing charters, shopping, dining

GALLAGHER HOUSE

Portland-on-the-Rideau

Portland-on-the-Rideau is a quiet community of historic homes on the shores of Big Rideau Lake. Founding father Albert Gallagher chose this site to establish numerous enterprises, among them a shipping company and lumber business. Gallagher doubled as reeve and postmaster, and built his elegant home in the centre of the action, across from the town wharf. That home is now an inn — Gallagher House — which is a good base from which to tour the region known as the Rideau Lakes.

This gracious home was built in 1910 from bricks manufactured on this very site. The inn was Gallagher's house, and in some senses, Portland was his town. From the spacious front verandah (well supplied with chairs for sidewalk supervisors), the innkeepers can point out Gallagher's original holdings: his store and bank across the street are still in commercial use, and his warehouse on the point is now a home. It is not a wonder, then, that his home dominates the main street of town, or that he could afford to equip it with deep wood trim and etched-glass transoms.

In taking on the restoration of Gallagher's house, John and Dianne Wright were well aware of his stature in the community. The house is decorated with old photographs of the days of Rideau Lakes shipping, and the guest rooms in the inn are named after steamships that would have tied up just across the street. Gallagher House proper has four rooms, some with private sink and toilet . All the rooms have gleaming maple floors, floral bedspreads and antique or reproduction furnishings, including porcelain wash basins. Three of the rooms share a large second-storey balcony, a wonderful place to take in the wide vista of Big Rideau Lake and watch cruisers come and go at the marina. The Rideau King room has a private balcony and fireplace.

Another family of importance, the Scovils, lived for years just down the street in a blue clapboard house (named after Peter Bresee, who built the house in 1844). That building is also a part of Gallagher House inn, and has four rooms and two suites. All rooms in Bresee House have full ensuite bathrooms, sitting areas with pull-out sofas, and queen-size beds. The Colonel By Suite is handicapped accessible and has a fireplace and a whirlpool tub.

Gallagher House is building its reputation around head chef David Blackburn, who prepares meals worth planning an entire vacation around; some diners claim that there is no better chef in Eastern Ontario. House specialties include oysters Rockefeller, gambas con limon (jumbo shrimp in a lemon and garlic sauce), and phyllo stuffed with Genoa salami, all of which are exquisitely prepared and presented. Blackened steak; salmon poached in court bouillion and served with a lime hollandaise; and pork tenderloin served on a bed of sun-dried tomatoes, guava and green peppers, are a few of the house entrees.

The other delightful side to meals at Gallagher House is the table service of innkeeper John Wright. Meal after meal brings a new round of jokes, anecdotes, and humorous introductions to the specials of the day.

Wright is also the breakfast chef. Eggs, Spanish omelets, French toast, granola and cereals are all well prepared, but the highlight of the morning meal is yogurt ananda, an ambrosial concoction of yogurt, fresh berries, honey and homemade granola. Sample it once and you will soon add it to your repertory of breakfast items at home.

John and Dianne Wright have an active program of special events for their guests, and given chef Blackburn's skill, it is not surprising that many of these festive occasions include special foods, such as elaborate, seven-course gourmet dinners, held on some weekends. Others, like the house patio parties, feature international barbecue foods (satays, steaks, grilled veggies) and feature "singing, dancing and loud carrying on." The Gallagher House has teamed up with Hart Breweries, in Carleton Place, to host a February beer-tasting feast, in which brews from microbreweries are served with a menu of appropriate gusto.

Gallagher House also organizes dinner cruises aboard the *Fathom Five*, a glass-bottomed boat. "Music on the Rideau," which involves a seven-course seafood dinner and a cruise serenaded by a string quartet, occurs two Wednesdays a month during the summer. Father's Day luncheon cruises are also offered.

Portland itself has a lot to offer travellers. The town has two small beaches and several interesting stores. During the winter, the ice on Big Rideau Lake is shovelled to create a large skating rink. The rest of the lake has good conditions for cross-country skiing. After ice break-up, maple syrup season arrives and the Millpond Conservation Area hosts special maple-related events. A trail along an abandoned railway line is used for hiking during the summer and skiing during the winter.

This region of Eastern Ontario is excellent territory for antique shopping. The area's deep historic roots mean that there are good sources of furnishings and domestic wares, and the distance from large cities means that prices are low. There are several shops within a short drive of Portland-on-the-Rideau; brochures listing shops and location are available from local merchants or from Gallagher House. Head north to Rideau Ferry, home of the famous Rideau Antiques. There are enough antiques, collector's items and conversation pieces on the front yard to keep you rummaging around for hours before you enter the old barn or the equally jam-packed house. The atmosphere at Glenburnie Antiques (a short drive west on the same road), is very refined; the shop specialty is elegant eighteenth- and nineteenth-century art and furnishings, from original paintings to silver serving dishes.

An excellent source for pre-Confederation Canadiana is Restoration Farms, near Athens. Furniture, tools, and domestic items are displayed in an 1845 farmhouse exactly as they would have appeared in a pioneer farmstead. Athens has made a place for itself in the hearts of daytrippers by commissioning artists to paint murals on buildings throughout town. Pick up a guide to the murals from the town hall, and take a walking tour of these large, well-executed artworks. My favourite is the one on the town high school entitled *Athens High School Graduation, 1921*. It depicts an old Model-T Ford, and, no matter what your position is relative to the painting, it appears as if the car is always facing you. Don't worry about appearing foolish as you walk back and forth in front of the school testing the power of this optical illusion — there will be other visitors engaged in the same endeavor.

The Rideau Lakes also have plenty of interest for the history buff. Any tour should take in the intriguing historic site at Jones Falls. The basis of the interest is a 19-metre-high, 107-metre-broad dam constructed by canal builder Colonel By. This was the first arched masonry dam in North America, and the largest in the world. Massive sandstone blocks were hand-cut to fit perfectly together without mortar. The dam is considered an engineering marvel to this day. Displays describe the hardships endured by workers constructing the dam and locks, and the technical triumph achieved in their construction. The Jones Falls site has a blacksmith shop and lockmaster's house, both with costumed interpreters ready to answer questions and provide tours. As with any locksite, Jones Falls makes a great picnic area; you can enjoy lunch while you oversee luxury cruisers and small pleasure craft navigating the locks.

Another good museum is located in the hamlet of Chaffey's Locks. Each lock on the Rideau waterway was supervised by a lockmaster who was responsible for lock operation, maintenance and military defense. The lockmaster's house is typically a white-frame cottage with a dark green roof and shutters. It is distinguished from other cottages by gun slits, a fireproof tin roof, and thick stone walls at ground level — reminders that the waterway was built as part of a defense against American attack, and that lockmasters were responsible for protecting their locks. A video at the museum presents an appealing portrayal of life in this tiny backwoods community, which continues to live in tune with the seasons, reaping the bounty of maple syrup and fish.

The Rideau Lakes region is a paradise for lovers of outdoor pursuits. The lakes are part of the Rideau Waterway, which is considered one of the most scenic and least crowded recreational waterways in the world. Boat rentals are available from marinas in Portland and other port towns, so you can do a little independent sailing, cruising or fishing.

Three provincial parks — Murphy's Point, Frontenac and Charleston Lake — have hiking trails that vary in length and degree of difficulty. The Rideau Trail is for long-distance backpackers; it runs from Kingston to Ottawa and contains some very challenging sections that are often wet. The trail is best accessed from Frontenac Park, where the staff provides trail maps and advice on conditions. Frontenac encompasses a huge region of rocky Canadian Shield scenery, and is known for its complete program of backwoods instruction. In the winter season, visitors may sign up for instruction and workshops on winter camping, snowshoeing and cross-country skiing. Murphy's Point and Charleston Lake parks are popular for swimming, as their shallow waters warm up to a pleasant temperature. Charleston Lake is also good for canoeing, and there are equipment rentals in the park.

Gallagher House and the Rideau lakes are a winning combination for travellers, with a highly enjoyable mix of historic sites, special events, country drives, and at the end of the day, a comfortable evening on the verandah after an excellent meal.

Gallagher House

14 West Water Street
Portland-on-the-Rideau, ON
(613) 272-2895
Fax: (613) 272-2897
Innkeepers: John and Diane Wright

10 rooms and suites
Dining room open to the public
Directions: Portland-on-the-Rideau is on Highway 15 between
    Smiths Falls and Gananoque.
Tariffs: inexpensive
On site: exercise room
Off site: antique hunting, Murphy's Point Provincial Park,
    Frontenac Provincial Park, Chaffey's Locks museum, boat
    cruises, boat rentals, cycling and mountain biking, cross-
    country skiing

TRINITY HOUSE INN

Gananoque

Quietly sauntering along the side streets of this attractive Thousand Islands town, you come across a solid, red-brick home — a squarely-built, nineteenth-century building that is commonly seen across the province. Respectable, even dignified, but not the stuff of fantasy. Since the sign outside indicates that this is an inn, you decide to open the door and have a look inside. You almost swoon with surprise, for you have been magically transported into the lap of Victorian splendour.

At Trinity House, the decor is not simply a backdrop, it's a scene-stealer. Lacquered Chinese screens, bronze herons, a Jacobean bench, a Rembrandt in an ornate golden frame, masses of fresh flowers everywhere…the eyes simply don't know where to begin. It's not that the house is overdone, it is elegantly and perfectly done, but with a flourish that few of us would attempt. The style is Victorian Chinois, chosen by innkeepers Jacques O'Shea and Brad Garside to create elegant accommodation that is an escape from the mundane.

Few of us would have seen the potential in the 1859 brick home of E. A. Atkinson, town doctor and founder of St. Lawrence Steel and Wire (which is still in operation). O'Shea and Garside, weary of Toronto and very much in love with the outstanding Thousands Islands sailing, decided to become innkeepers. All renovation, painting, decorating, re-carpeting and re-plumbing were accomplished by the innkeepers themselves — just ask to see the photo-album chronicles.

They created seven rooms — each named after a beloved St. Lawrence island — and one suite. The decoration in each room is highly individual, but each has bold wall colours, exquisite antiques, a private bath and full amenities, including a much-appreciated ironing board and iron. The Prince Regent suite is the stuff fantasies are made of: rough limestone walls, a wet bar with an enormous sun sculpture, a sitting room and a double whirlpool tub. The suite's basement location shields light sleepers from the hourly chimes of the town clock.

The main-floor lounge and two dining areas are decorated with vases overflowing with fresh flowers and have rare and priceless furnishings. The innkeepers were careful to respect the original elegance of the home; for example, the wide baseboards and cornice mouldings were retained and accented in white.

If you are looking for a home base to use while exploring the Thousands Islands region, look no farther than the town jail. Trinity House acquired Gananoque's first lock-up and sheriff's quarters, a picturesque limestone building just next door to the inn. It contains an apartment that accommodates four people, with full kitchen and dining facilities and a private balcony. The tin ceilings and stylish furnishings make this a perfect home away from home. The innkeepers are also in the process of restoring a riverside villa (an executive cottage in the heart of the islands) and an in-town bed-and-breakfast home.

Although Trinity House describes its cuisine as modern country house, the menu reflects the inn's eclecticism. All baking is done by the inn's own chef, and the inn's fine preserves are the creation of Garside's mother. Many of the summer vegetables are supplied by a local farmer and are raised organically.

Patrons favour the Danish Brie baked with a brown-sugar crust and served with fresh fruit, a tasty preface to chicken breast in a Mandarin curry sauce or pasticcio John Paul (linguini in a creamy sauce rich with smoked salmon, shrimp, parmesan and nutmeg). Desserts frequently include Balmoral pudding (a tribute to the region's United Empire Loyalist roots), seasonal fruit crumble and Georgian pecan flan. The inn's wine list — about sixty varieties at any one time — is carefully selected from estate offerings of limited vintages. The wine list, like the cuisine, borrows widely from around the globe, although Italian, Austrian and Canadian (particularly Cave Springs) wines are emphasized.

Guests may dine in the original parlour of the house or out on the renovated porch. The latter, with its tinkling fountain, is an ideal spot for a sunny breakfast. Warm-weather meals are best enjoyed on the back verandah, which overlooks the Trinity House gardens. Meticulous planning and immaculate grooming have produced a soothing haven of a garden that delights the senses. A waterfall cascades down a stone wall; roses, lilies and clematis burst forth in luxuri-ant blossom and perfume the air; and the whole delightful picture is framed with the graceful boughs of mature trees. Even the gar-den statuary appears to be smiling with approval. The gardens are a popular place for wedding ceremonies, and Trinity House is one host of the annual garden tour.

While the opulence of Trinity House is hard to leave, the Thousand Islands region has many intriguing possibilities for a day out. O'Shea and Garside can help plan a rewarding day of exploration. Reap the fruit of an active and sophisticated fine-arts and theatre community; take in a boat tour with its contrast of rocky islets and wind-twisted pine and the princely homes of tycoons; or bike along kilometres of scenic trails. Whatever your pleasure, the Thousand Islands has a day for you.

It was the beauty of the river, and the quality of its sailing that first attracted O'Shea and Garside to Gananoque in the first place. The name Trinity House, as mentioned in the inn literature, is borrowed from an old British term for corporations that provided naviga-tional aids in coastal waters. The inn owns a Grampian 30 sail-boat, which may be chartered by guests (groups of up to six or eight) for a personal tour with the innkeepers — a four-hour sail past the best scenery in the Thousand Islands, down wind to Ivy Lea and its famous international bridge, and back to Gananoque. Experienced sailors may even take a turn at the helm.

Those wishing to tour the islands under power may rent boats from local marinas or choose from several local cruise lines. All offer narrated cruises through the islands, and some include stops at Boldt Castle, on Heart Island. A short walk from Trinity House takes you to the Gananoque Boat Lines, which have the largest boats in the islands. Rockport is a small settlement in the heart of the islands. Its main attractions are the Andress boat works, the white-clapboard St. Brendan's Church, where mariners come by water for the blessing of the boats each spring, and two restaurants. Rockport is also the home of two more cruise lines. The Rockport Boat Line has two boats, and offers several cruises daily, and Heritage Boat Tours offers tours on two antique vessels.

No matter which cruise you take, you'll come away with an appreciation that the Thousand Islands have attracted the rich and famous for generations. Many of the mansions along the river and on the islands were built as summer homes. But the best of the lot for beauty and historic interest is in Brockville, a short drive east from Gananoque. Fulford Place was the home of native-son George Fulford, who made his fortune marketing "Fulford's Little Pink Pills" at the turn of the century. The riverside mansion and its eight thousand furnishings are now polished up for public display, and there are informative guided tours that describe the home and the lifestyle of the well-to-do during the early 1900s. The immense mahogany table is designed to seat forty-eight, and among regular dinner guests were the Prince of Wales and all but two twentieth-century Canadian Prime Ministers. Rooms are flamboyantly decorated in a variety of styles, from Tudor to French rococo, and have deeply carved panelling, Oriental carpets and Belgian silk tapestries.

Pleasure drivers will want to take in the entire St. Lawrence Parkway. The St. Lawrence Parks Commission has done an excellent job of providing picnic sites, beaches, boat launches and maps. Smart travellers will pick up a scrumptious picnic lunch at Gananoque's bakery, Ingrid's, and dine along the river. One of the nicest picnic sites is at Brown's Bay, where the shallow beach water warms up to a toasty temperature, and there's a wide-angle view of the river. Here too are historic displays, including the remains of a gunboat from the war of 1812 and exhibits that describe river ecology. An antique ferry (built in 1929) departs from the Brown's Bay dock, carrying daytrippers and campers to several islands of the St. Lawrence Island National Park.

A preferred way to observe life on the river is by cycling the Thousand Island bike path, which follows the river between Gananoque and Brockville. There is an excellent brochure for cyclists that interprets various natural and cultural features along the way. The pathway is rated as one of the top ten bike paths in Ontario.

Landon Bay is at the western end of the Parkway (and bikepath), and a relatively new facility, The Gardens at Landon Bay, is worth a visit. The 80-hectare property has a number of nature trails and gardens, and a varied program of interpretive walks and children's environmental day programs. One trail has a lookout over the St. Lawrence, and another passes by a beaver pond. There are gardens designed for butterflies and hummingbirds, a fern glen, a demonstration nut farm and a miniature Canadian bog. It's a good place to pick up ideas for the home garden, such as the various kinds of plants, nest boxes and shelter for birds, small mammals, reptiles and amphibians.

Take the time to explore the town of Gananoque. A re-created Victorian village is the highlight of the waterfront. It has several interesting shops, among them a bookstore and an art gallery, and contains the future site of a marine museum. The Gananoque Museum has displays of items collected over two centuries: furniture, dolls, clothing, photographs, and those famous antique St. Lawrence duck decoys.

The Thousands Islands Playhouse is located in a refurbished canoe club. It would be hard to imagine a more pleasant escape than an evening of light comedy, romance, music or mystery, followed by a leisurely stroll along the waterfront, where the lights of passing yachts move slowly under a canopy of stars. Trinity House provides a package that includes accommodation, meals, a boat cruise and theatre tickets, all at one reasonable price.

When ordinary life attempts to dull your senses, close your eyes, envisage Victorian opulence and exotic foods, click your heels three times and recite, "There's no place like Trinity House."

Trinity House Inn

Stone Street South
Gananoque, ON
K7G 1Z8
(613) 382-8383
1-800-265-4871 (Ontario only)
Fax: (613) 382-1599
Innkeepers: Jacques O'Shea and Brad Garside
Open April to December

8 rooms, one apartment
Dining room open to public, with reservations
Directions: Exit 645 south from 401; this is Stone Street and the
    inn is at number 90 South.
Tariffs: inexpensive
On site: spa services by arrangement, back garden
Off site: Thousand Islands Playhouse, Fulford Place, the Gardens
    at Landon Bay, shopping, boat cruises, pleasure driving,
    sailing, boating, fishing, hiking, cycling

DENAUT MANSION COUNTRY INN

Delta

There's a rule of thumb that it takes an innkeeper seven years of hard work to achieve a harmonious coordination of location, cuisine, facilities and guest services. But for David and Deborah Peets, it has taken just two short years of intensive preparations to arrive at something close to perfection — the Denaut Mansion Country Inn.

The object of their devotion is located in tiny Delta, a village off the beaten track in the Rideau Valley, northeast of Gananoque. Built of ochre sandstone in 1849, this mansion was the home of Walter Denaut, who had a notable career as a canal builder, merchant, post master and first reeve of the township. This prominent community figure entertained leaders such as John A.Macdonald, Charles Tupper, and Darcy McGee in his home. Denaut Mansion continues in the tradition of refined hospitality befitting the centre of social and economic life in the community.

The Peets have performed miracles of restoration. The first thing you'll notice upon entering the mansion is its bold, vibrant colours: the deep yellow of the entry, the brilliant cherry and plum in the dining room, the burnished amber of the red-pine floors. The second impression is the profusion of light, whether the morning sunlight that streams through the two-storey window in the stairwell, the late-afternoon sun that warms the buff stone of the old barn and makes the adjacent patio an ideal retreat, or the tree-filtered light of the portico. This airy character is enhanced by high ceilings and an uncluttered decor.

Every room of the inn is adorned with fine art and mementos of David and Deborah's world travels. Featured artists include Karen Falkenberg, from Kingston, and Martina Field, from Sharbot Lake. Note the wrought-iron chairs that sit under the painting of a Parisian bistro; they are the creation of local metalsmith Daniel Karem. The masterpiece of a hall table, with a smooth iron base and polished cherrywood surface, was a joint venture between Daniel and his carpenter brother Raphael. The Rideau Valley is, of course, popular antique hunting territory, and the Peets gleaned many of the inn's armoires, hutches, and the front-hall sofa, from nearby sales.

The living room, with its Runford fireplace and marble hearth, is a choice spot to read and relax after a day spent on the road or the trail. Deborah's sister created the mural in the dining room, which depicts the Jubilee block on the main street of Delta, circa 1930. The authenticity of the painting is verified by community elders, who can actually identify friends and relations in the sidewalk scene. The Traveller's Bar has burnt-orange walls and a stainless-steel countertop. Here, through his house cocktails and his own travel stories, David encourages guests to share their own travel adventures.

While the common rooms on the main floor express the lively and stylish character of the innkeepers, the four guest rooms and apartment, more subtle in decor, are spare, fresh and restful. The rooms are unique in furnishing and style, but each has an en suite bathroom, large windows set in deep window wells, and a view of lawns and immense old trees. The layout of the second storey means that there is little hall noise to disturb guests. The John A. room has a double bed so lofty that it comes with a step-stool for entry, and it is the only room with a tub and shower. The African room is decorated with souvenirs of the Peets's travels to that continent. The room named after Walter Denaut, with a reproduction Quebec wardrobe and a wrought-iron bed, has an early-Canadian air. But my personal favourite is the Coral Room. The bed has an eyelet bedskirt and a twig headboard, and the bed-side tables are actually statue bases from a church. With a seating area facing the back lawns, it is an ideal spot in which to revive yourself after a hectic work week.

The inn's separate two-storey apartment is a good option for families. The main floor has a full bath and kitchen, dining facilities, and a pull-out sofa. There is a queen-size bed in the master bedroom and a trundle bed in a smaller room for two kids; all are adorned with pioneer-style quilts. Kids can be left in the apartment with their own meal, which allows parents to fully enjoy Deborah's cuisine.

The Denaut Mansion sits on four hectares of lawn, woods and marsh that back onto the Rideau lakes. Future plans at the mansion include a canoe launch that will provide paddlers with access to the quiet waters and good bird-watching of Upper Beverly Lake. You don't need to travel far for a refreshing dip; just outside the living room is a pool, and there is an uncrowded beach at the town park.

The ever-thoughtful Peets have provided their own guide to local attractions in each guest room. David and Deborah are especially keen on serving guests interested in outdoor activities — biking, hiking, canoeing, and countryside rambles.

David, a keen cyclist himself, knows the country byways as well as anyone raised in the area, and has put admirable effort into discovering and documenting routes, which range from 25 to 100 kilometres in length. The Peets are happy to supply an ample picnic lunch, a detailed map and instructions. Low traffic levels and varied terrain make Eastern Ontario good cycling territory, and there is every expectation that Denaut Mansion will become favoured habitat for cycling clubs.

Eastern Ontario is just waking up to its fabulous potential for hikers. Close to Denaut Mansion is a trail along a railroad right-of-way; just ask David Peets to point out the way. For a more rigorous outing, exercise your soles on the famous Rideau Trail, a long-distance pathway between Kingston and Ottawa. There are many convenient access points, and again, your hosts have all the necessary directions. Several provincial parks are within convenient daytrip distance of the mansion, and all of them have very satisfying trails of various lengths and challenge. Closest to the inn is Charleston Lake Provincial Park, 2400 hectares of rocky Canadian Shield with facilities for hiking (independent and guided), swimming, canoeing and cross-country skiing. (The Peets can arrange for canoe rentals from outfitters near Charleston Lake or Frontenac Provincial parks.)

Murphy's Point Provincial Park, located near Westport, features one of Eastern Ontario's most unusual guided hikes. Phone ahead to reserve a spot on the afternoon Silver Queen Mine walking tour. At the mine entrance, you don a hard hat for a conducted tour of the abandoned mica mine; on the surface, you observe a reproduction of the miner's dormitory, and are allowed to take a piece of mica as a souvenir.

To revel in the crisp silver and blue of a Canadian winter, there's no better place than Frontenac Provincial Park. It is a forty-minute drive from the mansion, but it is well worth the extra travel time. Park staff offer superb winter programming, which includes skiing and snowshoeing instruction and guided treks for all levels, as well as winter camping and survival courses. The park is also popular for icefishing. The stillness of the Canadian Shield in winter is something that will bring you back for repeat visits. Cross-country ski buffs will want to find out about the 40 kilometres of trails maintained by the Triangle Ski Club. Skating on natural ice can't be beat, and the local ice rink is another active outdoors option available to wintertime guests of the Denaut.

Quieter pursuits described in the Denaut Mansion book of ideas include the Thousand Islands Playhouse in Gananoque (the innkeepers are pleased to arrange tickets); antique hunting along the backroads and in the local towns of Athens, Portland, and Rideau Ferry; and superb museums along the Rideau Canal. Somnolent Delta is worth an exploration, and the inn supplies a booklet that describes its historic buildings. The highlight is the lovingly restored Delta Mill (built in 1810), and its two storeys of exhibits on milling technology and local history. There are plans to have the mill in working order within the next few years.

There's nothing like a day in the great outdoors to work up an appetite, and no better home base to return to the Denaut. By dinnertime, the aroma of Deborah's kitchen wizardry wafts through the inn. She describes her style as fresh Mediterranean Californian, and it is obvious that the kitchen is intelligently informed by the Peets's travels. The dining room, open to the public evenings from Thursday to Saturday, has already gained a wide following for Deborah's flair.

Deborah always lays out a savoury spread. You might begin with subtly flavoured lentil cakes kept moist by an eggplant jacket that is neither wilted nor too crisp. The filet of salmon, served with a russet-coloured sauce, is redolent with cumin. An entree with such determined flavouring requires an accompaniment that doesn't retreat, and the crunchy Asian slaw of cucumber and cabbage certainly does the job. David does his part in the kitchen, too, with rich, custard-based ice creams and fresh sherbets that are served with fresh local fruit. The Denaut Mansion menu is filled with variety, featuring iced pea soup, coconut, shrimp and scallop stew with Israeli couscous, and plum gallette. The wine list includes domestic and foreign offerings, usually a half-dozen whites and reds and a couple of house wines.

Overnight guests awaken to a country-house breakfast. Serving time is flexible, but usually runs between 7:30 and 9:30. David produces the inn's own granola, müsli and gravlox, and the morning meal also includes seasonal fruit and berries, chocolate croissants, sweet loaves and baguettes. Many of the baked goods are fresh from the oven.

If the Denaut Mansion sounds too good to be true, the best is yet to come: the rates for rooms and dinner make the Denaut affordable enough for frequent visits. During the winter there are midweek specials, and there are midweek specials year round for the over fifty-five crowd.

David and Deborah Peets may be the new kids on the block among Ontario's innkeepers, but their creative genius and sincere care for their guests will ensure their continued success.

Denaut Mansion Country Inn

5 Mathew Street
Delta, ON
K0E 1G0
Tel & Fax: (613) 928-2588
Innkeepers: David and Deborah Peets

4 rooms and self-contained 2-bedroom apartment
Dining room open to public Thursday through Saturday
Directions: Delta is on Highway 42 between Smiths Falls and
    Gananoque. Signs in town lead to Denaut Mansion.
Tariffs: inexpensive
On site: gardens, woods, outdoor pool, canoeing
Off site: Delta Mill, Jones Falls, Kingston Mills, Thousand Islands
    Playhouse, Murphy's Point Provincial Park, antique hunting,
    canoeing, bird-watching, cycling, hiking, cross-country
    skiing, skating

28

SAM JAKES INN

Merrickville

The Rideau Waterway, from Ottawa to Kingston, is one of Canada's richest tourism resources. Sightseers travelling by water or by highway have access to exceptional historic sites and museums, pleasant waterfront scenery, villages with plenty of good shopping, and, in Sam Jakes Inn in Merrickville, a perfect place to call home.

Sam Jakes is Merrickville's pride and joy, a postcard-pretty stone building with green shutters, ornate gingerbreading, and a white fence with huge, round post heads. In 1861, Merrickville was a bustling canal town and commercial centre, and Sam Jakes was an important business figure and town benefactor. His main enterprise was the Jakes department store, which occupied the stone building at the corner of Main and St. Lawrence Streets. Any resident will inform you that Jakes's store was the largest mercantile between Chicago and Montreal. It even featured — a novelty at the time — an elevator. The home remained in the Jakes family until well into this century, but eventually fell into disrepair.

Innkeeper Gary Clarke, with long experience in heritage preservation and environmental work, valued the potential of this remarkable historic site. He had it designated a provincially significant heritage structure, and began restoration. The interior and exterior have great character, and are restored to look as they may have in Merrickville's heyday, the 1860s.

Perhaps the heritage theme is best seen in the dining room. The dining room has green wainscoting and striped wallpaper, tin wall sconces, and Queen Victoria scowls down from between twin candelabras. The tables have fresh flowers in vases made especially for the inn by local potter Stephen Sanger. During the summer, guests may dine in the backyard, surrounded by lilies and hosta, and shaded by trees and patio umbrellas.

In keeping with the innkeeper's interest in the heritage of Eastern Ontario, Cordon Bleu-trained chef Erick le Pors acts as an energetic culinary ambassador, travelling the countryside for the best possible local ingredients, which include Thistle Spring trout, Lanark pork, Moulton Hill veal, Levante Ranch emu, Cedar Ridge raspberries, Forfar cheddar and Mrs. McGarrigle's mustards. Homegrown Eastern-Ontario ingredients are used to produce a savoury squash, carrot and ginger soup; roast lamb with garlic and ginger compote; pork marinated with maple syrup and served with a zesty cranberry sauce; local rabbit stewed in Hart Amber Ale, with mushrooms and pearl onions; and a superb raspberry mousse cake. In the pub, the region's Scots heritage is manifested in single-malt whiskeys, and Hart Brewery in Carleton Place is the source of drafts and ales. Ontario wines are featured in the wine list.

An escape to Sam Jakes Inn wouldn't be complete without the Sunday brunch buffet. Large serving tables are piled high with salads (don't miss the best coleslaw in Ontario), smoked and marinated seafood and the inn's own baked goods, which are so popular they are available for sale. The carvery serves a roast of the day (turkey, ham or beef), as well as crepes, pancakes, sausage, bacon, hot vegetables and soup. The French toast, made with thick slices of oatmeal bread, deserves special mention. It is a challenge to leave room for the grand finale of cakes filled with fresh berries and drizzled with chocolate, puddings, fruit salad and cheesecake.

The inn guest rooms — twenty-four rooms and six suites — are located in a three-storey addition to the original Jakes home. The colour scheme is based on historically correct colours and fabric patterns, and the furnishings are a combination of antiques and locally made reproductions that are exact duplicates of those found in the Rideau Valley in the 1860s. There's no such thing as a standard room, since no two are identical. The suites have fireplaces and a seating area with armchairs; some have vaulted ceilings.

The inn basement has a sauna and health club, as well as a cosy library with a large stock of books and a crackling fire in the fireplace. Business facilities include what may well be the most beautiful meeting room among Ontario's inns. The room, with its original woodwork, has several huge windows that overlook the waterway. This, and additional meeting rooms, can be reserved for photogenic wedding ceremonies and receptions.

The staff at Sam Jakes make it easy for guests to enjoy the surrounding region, providing a wealth of information. There are cross-country skiing in the nearby Limerick Forest, and hiking on the Rideau Valley Walking Trail (the Ottawa–Kingston trail passes right through town), as well as boat cruises, golfing, horse-and-buggy rides and canoe routes. Staff can also provide suggestions on the best local sources of antiques and art. As an additional feature, the inn offers a plethora of packages at hard-to-resist prices.

The main draw for tourists in the region is the Rideau Waterway, where the rivers and lakes of two watersheds are linked by the Rideau Canal. The story of the canal's construction is one of the most profound in the nation's history; various chapters are recounted at the Parks Canada museums located at many of the lock stations along the waterway. Perhaps the best place to begin is at the Rideau Canal Museum, housed in a handsome stone mill complex in Smiths Falls. The museum lobby has a model of the canal, with its twenty-four lock stations and twenty-five dams. Details of its construction and navigation are provided via polished displays of photographs, text and artifacts. Conditions were nearly impossible for Colonel John By, as he struggled to adapt European engineering technology to fit Canadian topography and climate. His Irish-immigrant workers employed simple hand tools to carve this 200-kilometre path through forest, marsh and rock. Colonel By's masterpiece was not used for military purposes, as originally intended, but it did give birth to many canalside settlements that are the delight of locals and tourists alike.

To sweeten your getaway, visit the Hershey factory on the eastern edge of Smiths Falls. Follow the signs posted along Highway 43. You can't miss the plant — it has a giant Hersheybar on the roof. There are self-guided tours along a corridor with windows overlooking the production area. Visitors gaze down into deep vats of liquid chocolate and then follow the chocolate as it is transformed into popular treats, which move by the thousands along conveyor belts. The factory shop has great bargains on chocolate products of all sizes and shapes, individually priced or in bulk.

Driving east from Smiths Falls, the recommended route is to take Highway 43 until it meets up with Country Road 2, and then follow that north-shore roadway. Many Eastern-Ontario travellers name Burritts Rapids as the prettiest village along the Rideau. It would be hard to argue. It seems as if time has forgotten this little 1800s mill town, which is peaceful and orderly. A stroll along the back streets reveals houses and churches that have changed little in almost a century and a half. Burritts Rapids is the best place for a close look at a lock during operation. Lockmasters open and close the immense oak gates by hand-winch, as they have since Colonel By's days.

Kemptville is a good place to cross the river to the south side for your return. Drive south from town along Highway 44 and turn west along Bedell Road, toward Oxford Mills. On Bedell Road, stop in at Evergreen Farm, well known to viewers of CBC's *Midday* program as the home of Anstace and Larry Esmonde-White, gardeners extraordinaire. Evergreen Farm is open to the public, and green thumbs could easily spend a few happy hours here. The garden is divided into outdoor "rooms," each designed around a different theme. There's the blue and white garden, the scent garden, the rose garden, the shrub garden, and a splendid food-production area, with veggies, an orchard and herbs. The purpose of Evergreen Farm is not only to celebrate the joy of gardening, but also to provide instruction on topics such as composting, pruning, cold-frame use and tool selection.

It is indeed hard to leave Evergreen Farm, but unless you are permanently lost in the aromatic cedar maze, leave you must. The nearest town is somnolent Oxford Mills. The focal point of the town is a stone building — decked out with geraniums — built in 1842 as the town post office and general store. It is now the lively Brigadoon Restaurant, popular with cyclists and pleasure drivers who take afternoon tea or lunch on the outdoor patio.

Some visitors to Sam Jakes Inn never leave Merrickville — easily Eastern Ontario's nicest village — which has a winning combination of historic buildings and diverse shopping sure to win the heart of any daytripper. In the history department, the town has two interesting sites. The Colonel By Blockhouse Museum is the second-largest remaining blockhouse in Canada, and was built to protect the canal from attack. It is a curious structure with metre-thick stone walls on the first floor and a wooden upper storey. Inside, it presents the domestic life of a military officer and his family on the canal.

The blockhouse stands in a small riverside park, a pleasant place for a picnic or a treat from the Around the Corner bakery (a terrific little source of almond cream horns and butter tarts at what seem to be 1860s prices). Take the time to relax in the park and watch the traffic through the waterway. The water is always busy, with holiday houseboaters, speed boaters and anglers, all enjoying life on the river in their own way.

A fascinating facet of Merrickville's past has been given new life. In the centre of the Rideau River lies Pig Island, which was a bustling community of fifty-eight foundries and factories. Now called the Merrickville Industrial Ruins, the stone remains of these businesses are a poignant reminder of days gone by.

Much of Merrickville's charm comes from its fine, stone commercial buildings, many of which are now shops stocked with fine art, crafts and clothing. There is such a variety of wares that there is sure to be something to keep every member of the family amused. Some of the village mainstays include Village Metalsmiths (custom metal signs and Victorian reproductions), Waterway Studio, Wood-N-Feathers (with everything for birdlovers, from feeders to sculptured birds), Mirick's Landing Country Store (folk art, souvenir clothing and country decorator accents), and a personal favourite, the Hot Glass Studio, where beautiful blown-glass objets d'art are produced before your very eyes.

Sam Jakes Inn, in decor and cuisine, is deeply rooted in the cultural heritage and natural environment of the Rideau Valley. Perhaps that is why it continues to flourish. Put down some Rideau roots of your own by enjoying the hospitality offered here.

Sam Jakes Inn

118 Main Street East
Merrickville, ON
K0G 1N0
(613) 269-3711
(614) 1-800-567-4667
Fax: (613) 269-3713
Innkeeper: Gary Clarke

30 rooms
Dining room open to public
Directions: The inn is in central Merrickville.
Tariffs: inexpensive
On site: sauna, exercise room
Off site: Rideau Canal Museum, Hershey Factory, shopping, boat
    cruises, antique hunting, boating, fishing, swimming,
    cycling, canoeing, cross-country skiing

29

THE CARMICHAEL INN & SPA

Ottawa

Ottawa is not only one of the world's most beautiful capital cities, but it is also an inviting holiday destination, with dozens of galleries and historic sites and many opportunities for outdoor activity in a beautiful riverside location. Many attractions are centrally located, and may be visited on foot or by bicycle along Ottawa's many traffic-free pathways. The Carmichael Inn & Spa, a hospitable and luxurious alternative to large hotels, is perfectly located near galleries, museums, historic sites and the beautiful Rideau Canal.

The Carmichael is a fine example of the Queen Anne architecture favoured by the wealthy at the turn of the century, with fanciful turrets, gables, tall chimneys and an enormous curved porch. The house was built in 1901 for wine merchant Newell Bates, and over the decades it has been the home of business leaders and a Supreme Court judge, and has even served as a convent. Renovations have added modern facilities to the house while retaining its original elegance.

Although newly opened, the Carmichael has all the earmarks of an excellent hostelry. Innkeeper Brian Fewster began his hospitality career at Sir Sam's Inn, where he quickly became addicted to innkeeping. He has successfully translated Sir Sam's relaxed yet sophisticated ambience to an urban setting. That country-inn atmosphere sets The Carmichael apart from big city hotels, and has made this a preferred home base among business travellers visiting Ottawa. The Carmichael is known not only as a country inn, but also as a popular spa that pampers guests and local residents alike.

The Carmichael Inn is named for Franklin Carmichael, a member of the illustrious Group of Seven. The inn is rich in Canadian artwork, with numerous prints from the Group of Seven and fine main-floor displays from contemporary artists in a variety of media. There are eleven rooms, which are not large, but are comfortably furnished with antiques and queen-size beds and decorated in subtle florals and plaids in the inn's signature green and burgundy. The eye-catching furniture includes enormous armoires and carved headboards. Many rooms have writing tables and wing chairs, and several have gas fireplaces and whirlpool tubs. The rooms facing Cartier Street offer a terrific view of the Church across the street and one of the third-storey rooms has a triple skylight and a deep Japanese soaking tub. The spacious main-floor suite has luxurious furnishings and a large bathroom with a whirlpool tub. This suite doubles as a meeting room for small business functions, and what a nice change it makes from impersonal hotel settings.

Before heading off for a day of meetings or sight-seeing, guests partake of a full continental breakfast — cereals, yogurt, fruit and baked goods. Business visitors appreciate being able to walk to their appointments, and the innkeepers can help leisure travellers arrange for skate and bike rentals, walking tours and other activities. The inn is a stone's throw from the pathways along the Rideau Canal, which makes it easy to begin or end a day with rollerblading, cycling or an invigorating skate along the world's longest natural skating rink. The Inn is in a prime location for enjoying all the festivities that mark February's Winterlude, where ice sculpting competitions, food vendors and live entertainment vie for the attention of the thousands of locals and tourists who skate on the canal.

After a full day of touring or business, there's nothing better than the Carmichael's spa treatments to relax and rejuvenate. The spa is located in the inn's lower level, which makes it well-insulated against traffic and lobby intrusions. The warm Mediterranean colour scheme, and the sounds of trickling water and soft background music contribute to the spas sense of escape.

Spa treatments are offered by a staff of three specialists who run a program around three themes: massage, body care, and hydrotherapy. Massage choices include traditional Swedish and Shiatsu, as well as reflexology and aromatherapy. Three types of body wraps — herbal, mud and seaweed — rejuvenate the body, eliminating toxins, and cleansing and nourishing the skin. The hydrotherapy is designed to take away the cares of the day, and the lighting, temperature and water jets are adjusted to your own preferences. Three types of hydrotherapy are offered: fango mud (volcanic mud), milk whey (great for the skin dried by central heating and Canada's cold) and seaweed (which nourishes the skin).

Spa treatments can be enjoyed individually, or, for a really thorough pampering, taken as part of a full day at the spa. A spa day, a popular gift item, includes a choice of three treatments, a nutritious light lunch, afternoon tea and fruit juices throughout the day. Robes and slippers are available for lounging between treatments. Some visitors enjoy the spa and inn so much that they stay several days longer than they had planned.

The first item on the agenda of most capital-region visitors is a trip to Parliament Hill, which comprises three buildings: Centre Block (the House of Commons and the Senate) and the East and West Blocks (where MPs have their offices). Parliament Hill is not hard to find; most streets in the downtown lead to the Hill's spectacular clifftop setting high above the Ottawa River. The walk from the Carmichael may be lengthy for some, but is very pleasant if you take the pathways along the Rideau Canal. Excellent Parliament Hill tours (in English and French) are offered daily during the summer and must be reserved at the striped Infotent just beside the Centre Block. During the winter, arrange for a tour at the Visitor Welcome Centre, located near the main entrance to Parliament.

There are actually three different Hill tours: Centre Block (the most popular), Parliament Hill Out of Doors, and East Block. Centre Block tours focus on the historic and architectural features of the House of Commons and the Senate chambers, and include a brief overview of Canadian civics. The tour highlight is the Senate library, a beautiful room with three storeys of book shelves, wrought-iron staircases and superb wood-carving. Tours conclude with an elevator ride to the top of the Peace Tower for a view of the river and Parliament Hill.

A little-publicized but highly recommended tour is the one that reveals the inner sanctums of East Block. Several rooms have been restored to their 1872 condition, among them the offices of Sir John A. Macdonald, Sir George Etienne Cartier and Governor General Lord Dufferin. The Privy Council Chamber, where the cabinet met, is properly formal, with an enormous chandelier that weighs 180 kilograms, and plenty of painting and gilding. Take a look at the shelves of legal texts — some of them are over four hundred years old.

During the summer, time your visit to Parliament Hill to coincide with the Changing of the Guard ceremony at 10 A.M. Colour, music and flawless execution characterize this presentation designed to thrill any lover of pageantry. Summer evenings are enlivened by sound and light shows, which take place in the Centre Block. These performances bring the Parliament Buildings to life, with taped voices, floodlights and sound effects. The bells of the Peace Tower are featured during carillon concerts, and during summer afternoons, short scenes from Canadian history are enacted on the Parliament lawn.

Nation building hasn't been all cabinet reports and court decisions. The real heart of Canadian history has more to do with creating communities in a landscape of rock, water and snow. It seems very appropriate, then, that the truly rugged side of Canadian life has a memorial at the very heart of our capital. The Bytown Museum is dramatically set deep in a rocky cleft that separates Parliament Hill from the Chateau Laurier. The building was the commissariat of canal-builder Colonel By, and is Ottawa's oldest stone building. Text, artifacts and excellent audio-visual displays portray By as a hero of engineering who grappled with the challenging Canadian environment. Equally tough were his Irish-immigrant workers, who used hand tools to hack a canal out of bedrock and swamp, fighting malaria, cold and accidents along the way. Right outside the door of the museum stand eight locks created from the rock on this very site. This is the perfect place to survey the luxury cruisers as they wait their turn to enter the Rideau Canal, which is considered one of the world's best pleasure waterways.

To gain a glimpse of nineteenth-century homelife, head for Laurier House (on Laurier Avenue East, a good walk from The Carmichael). Sir Wilfrid Laurier lived in this yellow Italianate-style home from 1897 until 1919, and it was the home of William Lyon Mackenzie King from 1923 until 1950. Tours provide fascinating accounts not only of the house itself, but also of the lives of its notable residents. Several second-floor rooms are furnished with Laurier's own belongings and feature elegant oak panelling and carving. The highlight of a Laurier House tour for most visitors will be Mackenzie King's study, which has a portrait of the Prime Minister's mother (apparently the medium for communion between the two), King's infamous crystal ball, and a guest book signed by the rich and famous of the day.

Ottawa's abundance of first-rate art galleries and museums is now receiving the attention it deserves — some visitors come to the capital for the artwork alone. The greatest concentration of galleries is in the Sussex Street-Byward Market area, just a few blocks from Parliament Hill (and a pleasant bike ride from the Carmichael Inn). Moshe Safdie's magnificent glass edifice is the perfect home for the extensive National Gallery. Nineteen hundred works from around the world and across the centuries are on display. The Canadian Museum of Caricature is just across Sussex Street from the National Gallery. Political cartoons from the National Archives are displayed, and both the art and biting satire make this a worthwhile visit. Also in the neighbourhood is the Canadian Museum of Contemporary Photography, which is tucked into a pleasant nook between the Chateau Laurier and the Rideau Canal. Changing exhibits of historic and contemporary works are displayed in an environment especially designed to show photographs off to best advantage.

Whether you travel to our beautiful capital on business, or are taking in the sites as part of a holiday, The Carmichael Inn's quiet atmosphere, therapeutic spa treatments, and superb location make it a capital choice among accommodations.

The Carmichael Inn & Spa

46 Cartier Street
Ottawa, ON
K2P 1J3
(613) 236-4667
Fax: (613) 563-7529
Innkeeper: Brian C. Fewster

11 rooms
Breakfast only
Directions: Exit Highway 417 at Metcalfe Street, drive north to
    Somerset and then east to Cartier.
Tariffs: moderate
On site: spa services
Off site: Parliament Buildings, National Gallery of Art, Colonel
    By Museum, Chinatown, guided bus tours, cycling,
    shopping, skating